SAVOR A TASTE
of the California Desert

DESERT SPRINGS PUBLISHING
CUSTOM BOOKS

78-365 Highway 111, Suite 340, La Quinta, California 92253

Text Copyright © 2008 by Victoria J. Bailey / All Photographs © 2008 by Victoria J. Bailey

Library of Congress Cataloging-Publication Data on file with the Publisher.
Savor A Taste of the California Desert, Signature Restaurant Recipes
Cookbook: recipes from the acclaimed California Desert Resorts' Restaurants.

ISBN 0-97275725-2
ISBN 978-0-9727572-5-6

Publisher and Editorial Director: VICTORIA J. BAILEY — victoria@desertspringspublishing.com
Food Stylist/Editor and Hospitality Consultant: KIM K. CRANDAL — kimcrandal@aol.com
Cover and Book Design: THOMAS GRANADE DESIGN — thomasgranade@mac.com
Custom Photography: MARK CIESLIKOWSKI — eventimages@dc.rr.com
Editorial Consultant: GAYL BIONDI

For information about special discounts for bulk purchases,
contact Desert Springs Publishing Custom Books at 760-219-7008
or orders@desertspringspublishing.com

www.desertspringspublishing.com
www.savorataste.com

Printed in China / First Printing, 2008

❖ FOREWORD ❖

To live in the California desert resort communities of the Coachella Valley is to be awed by the beauty of nature, to share in an eclectic blend of cultures and sensibilities, and to perfect the art of fine living through fine dining. We go out with family and friends to dine at our favorite restaurants because they feel like home.

Great restaurants, like great homes, have a character all their own. *SAVOR A TASTE* of the California Desert celebrates the genuine hospitality of hosts and restaurateurs, and the culinary artistry of chefs who craft the sensual delights of perfectly-prepared food that makes for a memorable dining experience.

While culinary professionals are proud of all their creations, oftentimes one signature dish comes to represent a particular chef and the restaurant with which he or she is affiliated. It is these uniquely original straight-from-the-heart dishes to which this book is dedicated.

We've collected a bounty of one-of-a-kind recipes — some traditional, some unexpected — that epitomize our casually elegant California desert resort lifestyle. With these recipes, the chefs display their personal tastes and sense of artistic flair. We encourage you to visit all of the featured restaurants. You'll find their contact information in the back of the book.

It was a true pleasure getting to know the eclectic mix of chefs who contributed to this volume. As they would all tell you, there's no greater joy than sharing great food and great conversation with the people you care about. So, have some fun in the kitchen and make some memories of your own.

Turn the page and allow us to introduce you to the talented people who made this book possible. They represent restaurants in Palm Springs, Cathedral City, Rancho Mirage, Palm Desert, Indian Wells, La Quinta and Indio.

Victoria and Kim

(TOP PHOTO - from left to right)

Mitch Harper, Eldon Pico, Kathy Maddox, Jim Shiebler, Jose Montejano, Marilyn Estenson, William Withrow, Luis Zamora, Mario Marfia, Alfonso Fong, Guillermo Avalos, Pierre Pelech.

(BOTTOM PHOTO - from left to right)

Samantha Ward, Michel Schenker, Patricia Hook, Mary McGowan, Bill Beck, Richard Riccio, Danny Riccio, Rob Wilson, Arthur L. Vasques, Peter Harbur, Milan Tojagic, Jorge Villabona.

Adobe Grill

La Quinta Resort & Club

✦ Grilled Lamb Chops Toluca Style

SERVES 4

12 Colorado lamb chops,
    3 ounces each
2   tablespoons vegetable oil
Salt and pepper

Marinade:
4   tablespoons achiote paste
4   whole cloves roasted garlic
1   teaspoon fresh rosemary
2   cups cider vinegar

Sauce:
1 ½ cups of demi glaze
1 ½ teaspoons fresh rosemary
1   teaspoon fresh thyme
1   teaspoon garlic, chopped
3   bay leaves
4   tablespoons onions, diced
¼   cup Roma tomatoes
1   ancho dried chile
½   cup red wine
Salt and pepper

Potatoes:
4   pounds russet potatoes,
    peeled
½   cup ground chorizo, cooked
½   cup roasted corn
¾   cup heavy cream
Salt

Garnish:
¾   cup fresh spinach
1   tablespoon vegetable oil
1   tablespoon garlic, chopped
½   cup ranchero or cacique
    cheese
4   sprigs fresh rosemary

How fitting that we begin our book highlighting dining in the desert and those who make it happen with the Adobe Grill. The restaurant is named after the 100,000 adobe clay bricks used to build the famed La Quinta Hotel in 1926, which is now the La Quinta Resort & Club™. Reigning atop the plaza overlooking winding pathways, tranquil streams of running water and those magnificent flower gardens, you will find the Adobe Grill.

The authentic décor and South American music sets the stage for an enchanting evening. Offering traditional regional Mexican cuisine, signature dishes include authentic moles, tableside guacamole, Halibut Empanisado and, of course, their Grilled Lamb Chop Toluca Style.

Whether vacationing in our desert or just stopping by to enjoy one of their classic jumbo margaritas, this is a place to truly savor a taste of Mexico. Chef Jose Montejano and the whole team at Adobe Grill offer an enthusiastic, "Bienvenidos!"

Method —

Marinade: Mix achiote paste, roasted garlic, rosemary and vinegar in a non-reactive bowl. Marinate lamb chops overnight.

Sauce: Combine all ingredients in a saucepan and mix (with the exception of the demi glaze). Bring to a boil and reduce to half. Add the demi glaze. Simmer for 5 minutes. Strain sauce and season with salt and ground black pepper.

Reduce heat and cover to keep warm.

Potatoes: Boil potatoes until done. Brown chorizo about 10 minutes. Add remaining ingredients and mash together until a creamy consistency is established.

Garnish: Sauté vegetable oil, garlic and spinach until spinach wilts down. Keep warm.

Chops: Heat the grill to high. Remove chops from marinade and brush on both sides with oil and season with salt and pepper. Place on the grill and grill until golden brown and slightly charred, 3 to 4 minutes. Flip the chops over and continue grilling to medium-rare, about 2 to 3 minutes. Let rest 5 minutes before serving. Top with spinach and cheese, garnish with rosemary sprig.

Wine and Spirit Pairing —
Opolo Mountain Red Zinfandel

Amorè

Ristorante Italiano

SERVES 6

- 2 ½ cups Maine lobster claw and knuckle meat
- 5 gallons water
- 3 pounds Idaho potatoes, peeled and cut into ¼ cubes
- 2 ½ cups plus 3 tablespoons kosher salt
- 1 ¼ cup garlic cloves
- 2 cups heavy cream
- 2 eggs
- 5 ½ cups all purpose flour
- 2 ⅔ cups extra virgin olive oil
- 1 cup gorgonzola cheese
- ½ cup fresh basil, chopped
- 4 cups peeled can tomatoes
- ½ teaspoon black pepper
- 2 tablespoons ground paprika
- ¼ teaspoon ground cayenne
- ¼ teaspoon ground cardamom
- 6 Maine lobster tails, 4 ounces each
- ¾ cup unsalted butter
- 2 ¼ cups white cooking wine
- Daikon sprouts, enoki mushrooms, green chives

❖ Lobster Gnocchi

A delightful dining experience begins at Amorè before even entering the front door. This architectural masterpiece is one of the most unique in the desert.

Once inside, there are great views of the Santa Rosa Mountains from almost every table where you can watch the sunset or turn your attention to the action in the open exhibition style kitchen. It is here that Chef Luis Zamora and his team skillfully prepare some of the finest authentic Italian food in the desert. We recommend ordering the "must try" appetizer Eggplant Rotilini while looking over the rest of the menu to select your entrée from the many over-the-top choices. Their featured dish, Lobster Gnocchi, deserves your attention.

Method —

Gnocchi: Boil potatoes in 1½ gallons of water and ½ cup kosher salt for 30 minutes or until soft. For roasted garlic, sauté over medium heat 1 cup olive oil and ¾ cup garlic cloves until they become soft. Do not overcook. Place garlic in a blender along with 2 tablespoons of oil and puree to a smooth consistency. Strain the potatoes, rinse with cold water, mash in a mixer or with a potato masher, and add the puree of roasted garlic, 1 cup heavy cream and 2 tablespoons of kosher salt. Refrigerate for 90 minutes. Place mashed potatoes in a large bowl. Slowly add eggs, mixing with a spoon. Using 4 ½ cups of flour, add the flour 1 cup at a time. The dough should be sticky, but should not stick to your fingers. On a floured cutting board (2 cups flour or more if needed) roll out dough. Cut the dough into 4 quarters to make it easier to work with. Cut dough into ½ inch cubes. Bring 3 to 4 gallons of water and 2 cups kosher salt to a boil. Add the potato dumplings and boil for 5 minutes. Strain with cold water and toss them in 1 cup of olive oil. Refrigerate until ready to use or add to the sauce immediately and serve.

Sauce: Sauté ½ cup sliced garlic with ⅓ cup olive oil until golden brown. Add ½ cup basil and 1 cup gorgonzola until the cheese melts. Blend 4 cups peeled can tomatoes, 1 cup heavy cream and add to cheese mixture. Let it reduce 10%. Add the 18 ounce lobster claw and knuckle meat, season with 1 tablespoon salt and ½ teaspoon pepper. Combine with the gnocchi.

Lobster: Pre-heat your oven to 350°F. Cut the back of the lobster shell to pull out the meat and place "piggy back" on shell. Sprinkle the meat with 2 tablespoons paprika, ¼ teaspoon cayenne and ¼ teaspoon cardamom and top each tail with 1 ounce of butter. Bake with wine in a non-stick shallow pan for 6-8 minutes.

Wine & Spirit Pairing –
Antinori - Cervaro della Sala Chardonnay

11

Arnold Palmer's

Fish:
6 sea bass filets, 6 ounces each

Marinade:
1 cup honey
1 cup light soy sauce
¾ cup white wine vinegar
¾ cup canola oil

Stir-fry:
½ cup carrots, julienne
½ cup zucchini, julienne
½ cup red bell peppers, julienne
½ cup beans sprouts
1 cup rice noodles, pre-cooked
¼ cup cilantro and basil, chopped together

❖ Chilean Sea Bass

Arnold Palmer's Restaurant is a true reflection of the man himself. The restaurant is classy and elegant with a touch of warmth you might find in your own home. The walls are covered with mementos, trophies, and pictures of Arnie's life and triumphs.

While the genuine comforts and traditional clubhouse style surrounds you, there is also a finely manicured nine-hole putting green to pass time between courses. There are stunning views of the Santa Rosa Mountains, cozy fireplaces in each room, courtyard ambience, five separate dining rooms, a wine cellar with over 300 varieties and a popular bar with nightly entertainment.

The menu is actually three in one. It consists of Steak House Selections, Chef's Features and Arnie's Favorite comfort foods. The Sea Bass recipe selected by Chef Brett Maddock is light and a great dish for the desert. "Cooking fish is what I enjoy and there are many ways to prepare it," says Maddock.

Method —

Marinade: Place all ingredients in a blender and blend for 1 minute. Put marinade in a plastic container and set aside. Marinade can be made up to 10 days in advance.

Fish: Pre-heat oven to 300°F. With olive oil and a non stick sauté pan, sear sea bass on one side until it is browned, place in a baking dish and pour marinade on top — enough to cover ¼ of the fish. Place the dish in the oven for about 7 minutes. A great tip is to use a toothpick in the center of the fish. If it goes in easy it is done.

Stir-fry: In a wok or sauté pan, sauté the vegetables in a little sesame oil until tender. Cook these very hot and fast. Toss in noodles and chopped herbs, and add a spoon of marinade to mixture creating a glaze on your vegetables. Place stir-fry in the center of each bowl and lay the fish on top. Strain marinade and pour it on top of the fish. Garnish the fish with fresh basil and cilantro.

Note: Rice noodles can be found at Asian markets and specialty stores. Cook them like pasta. To julienne vegetables, cut them into match stick-size strips. The fish marinade is great with cod, halibut or any white flakey fish. The sea bass is a mild flavored fish and stays moist after cooking.

Wine & Spirit Pairing —
"Parentai" Sauvignon Blanc, from the Matua Valley of New Zealand

Brett P. Maddock

Azur

La Quinta Resort & Club

✦ Braised Irish Salmon

SERVES 4

4	salmon filets, 7 ounces each
1	quart chicken stock
1	pint coconut milk
2	teaspoons honey
½	pound ginger
½	pound lemongrass
½	cup ponzu sauce
2	pounds Okinawa purple sweet potatoes
1	cup all purpose flour
2	egg yolks
½	cup grated parmesan
1	pound snow peas, julienned
1	teaspoon butter
½	cup extra virgin olive oil
1	teaspoon piment d'Espelette powder
¼	cup daikon sprouts

Salt and pepper

Tucked inside the historic La Quinta Resort & Club™ is their flagship restaurant where extraordinarily elegant and romantic dining experiences prevail. Chef de Cuisine William Withrow describes his French-European inspired cooking methods as California-International cuisine, saying, "I love to prepare classics with a twist and having our menu reflect fresh seasonal products and specialty items."

Culinary expectations continue to be raised at AZUR with their recent addition of a terrific sushi bar in the lounge area and a series of wine dinners to showcase their extensive wine list, acclaimed by *Wine Spectator* magazine. Maitre d' Karel Vidlak oversees the professional service staff that tends to every detail, further enhancing AZUR's unique atmosphere.

Chef Withrow shares with us this classic dish with a twist.

Method —

Broth: Bring chicken stock with ginger and lemongrass to a boil and simmer for ½ hour. Strain and reserve half of the chicken stock. Add coconut milk and honey to the other half and reduce by half, season with salt and pepper to taste.

Gnocchi: Bake sweet potatoes. Remove from oven, and while still warm, peel and rice onto a flat surface. Creating a well, add parmesan and egg yolks in center. Slowly incorporate flour to form the dough, knead very gently, patting and pressing the dough with your hands until all the flour is incorporated. Add additional flour to obtain a fairly firm, smooth, non-sticky dough. Roll into logs and cut dough into 1-inch pieces. Poach in boiling salted water and cook until they float, about 1 minute. As gnocchi float to top of boiling water, remove them to ice bath. Continue until all have been cooled off. Let sit several minutes in bath and drain from ice and water.

Fish: Pre-heat oven to 400°F. Place salmon in a baking dish and add the remaining chicken broth. Bake for 8 minutes. Meanwhile, sauté snow peas in butter, and reheat gnocchi in coconut broth.

Blend olive oil and piment d'espelette powder in a blender until oil is bright red.

Note: Okinawa purple sweet potato, ponzu sauce and piment d'espelette power can be found at your local specialty grocery store.

Wine & Spirit Pairing —
2003 Conundrum Chardonnay

Babe's

Bar-B-Que Grill & Brewhouse

SERVES 4

1   2-pound pork tenderloin

Special Cole Slaw:
2   pounds green cabbage, shredded
1   red bell pepper, thinly sliced
1   cup mandarin orange segments
1   cup sliced local Deglet Noor dates or hydrated raisins
2   bunches green onions, thinly sliced
1   cup candied pecans
Poppy seeds and black sesame seeds to taste

Gastrique (Glazed Reduction):
8   cups apple cider vinegar
2   cups sugar

Who else but veteran restaurateur Don Callender, founder of the highly-acclaimed Marie Callender's, could pull off placing three 800-pound bronze pigs outside his BBQ restaurant, in the heart of Rancho Mirage?

Babe's is not only the largest BBQ restaurant in the desert, but the micro-brewery has won gold, silver & bronze medals at competitions such as the Great American Beer Festival, the Australian International Beer Awards and California State Fair. With great patience and pride, they smoke their pork, chicken and beef with 100% hickory logs in a rotisserie smoker.

Executive Chef/GM, Arthur L. Vasquez, proudly shares that, "It is all these things that make us unique to the desert and one of the best American BBQ experiences in the Coachella Valley!"

Method —

Gastrique: To prepare your gastrique, combine cider vinegar and sugar in a deep saucepan. Bring to a boil, stir until sugar is diluted, reduce heat to medium and let simmer for 15 to 20 minutes. Set aside to cool. Place in the refrigerator until you are ready to make your slaw. For best results do this the day before.

Pork Tenderloin: Season tenderloin with salt and a generous amount of fresh ground pepper.

In a charcoal grill, place your briquette coals on one half of the grill and light. Take 2 to 3 pounds of hickory wood chips and soak in water for approximately 30 minutes. Allow the charcoal briquettes to burn down to a white-colored ash. Before cooking, drain the hickory chips and place them on the coals. Wait 3 to 5 minutes after adding hickory chips to the coals before placing tenderloin(s) on grill grate opposite the coals. Close the grill cover. Using indirect heat allows the meat to cook slowly. There will be no need to turn the meat using this method. If the grill temperature exceeds 275°F, open the grill cover or smoker, let some of the heat escape, then replace grill cover until the tenderloin reaches an internal temperature of 170°F. Let the tenderloin rest for 3 to 4 minutes. Slice very thin and serve on top of cole slaw.

Special Slaw: Mix all cole slaw ingredients in a large bowl with 8 ounces of cold gastrique and mix well. For best results mix slaw 10 to 15 minutes before you are ready to use it. Do not prepare slaw more than 1 hour beforehand.

Wine & Spirit Pairing
La Crema Pinot Noir from the Russian River Valley

Babe's Jack-A-Lope Ranch

❖ John Wayne Chili & Cornbread

SERVES **6**

Chili:
- 3   27-ounce cans ranch style beans
- 1   15-ounce can diced tomatoes in juice (use the juice)
- 1   15-ounce can roasted bell peppers (red or yellow), diced
- 2   cups beef broth
- 1   cup mild enchilada sauce
- 2   packets Lawry's taco seasoning
- 1   tablespoon brown sugar
- ½   tablespoon ground cumin
- 1   yellow onion, diced
- 1   garlic clove, chopped
- 1   pound lean ground beef or ground turkey
- 1   tablespoon sweet Italian sausage seasoning

Skillet Cornbread:
- 1   cast iron skillet, (12-inch) well-seasoned
- 4   cups Marie Callender's cornbread mix
- ½   cup granulated sugar
- 2   cups water
- ½   cup frozen roasted corn and bell pepper medley
- 1   cup cream corn
- 1   small can diced Ortega mild green chilies

Honey Butter:
2 part soft unsalted butter
1 part honey, whip until smooth

Don Callender has gone all out creating a restaurant like none other. Inspired by the tropical ambiance of his own back yard full of bronzed animals, water features and lush foliage, Babe's Jack-A-Lope Ranch is situated on almost 10 acres and has five dining areas, two bars, a game room, outside patio area, deck with fire pits and a take-out area in addition to banquet facilities. This showcase venue features the same popular Bar-B-Que & Brewhouse menu and award winning micro-brews enjoyed at Babe's in nearby Rancho Mirage.

"People who are aware of me know I'm half crazy." said Callender, age 80, who insists this will be his last, and greatest, foodservice development of the many he has launched in his 60-year career focusing on innovation and quality.

There is something about the mythical jack-a-lope that conjures up visions of the old west, cowboys, campfires and John Wayne. The John Wayne Turkey Chili and Skillet Corn Bread is our featured recipe.

Method —

Chili: Mix sausage seasoning together with ground meat and brown in a large pot at medium-high heat. Remove the meat and set aside. Do not drain. Sauté the diced onions and chopped garlic clove in the same pot at medium heat for 5 minutes. Add the cooked meat back in with the beans, tomatoes, bell peppers, broth, and enchilada sauce. Stir and cook for another five minutes. Add the taco seasoning and brown sugar. Reduce heat to low and simmer for 20-30 minutes. Season with salt and pepper to taste.

Skillet Cornbread: In a mixing bowl combine all ingredients and mix for 1 minute. Spray two 2-inch cast iron skillets or one 12-inch skillet with a butter flavored non-stick spray. Pour the corn bread mixture into the skillets 1½ inch from the top. Bake in a preheated 380°F oven for 25-30 minutes, until cornbread is golden and tests done. For an extra touch, brush on melted honey butter for sweetness and shine

Note: If a cast iron pan ever begins to show signs of rusting or imparts a metallic taste, it will need to be re-seasoned. Scour the pan well with steel wool and wash with soapy water. Rinse, dry thoroughly, then coat with shortening or oil and place in a 250°F oven for about 2 hours. Wipe with paper towels to absorb any excess oil, and it's ready to use. Never put iron pots in the dishwasher.

Wine & Spirit Pairing —
Babe's "29 Palms" Pale Ale

Café des Beaux-Arts

6 duck magrets, 6 ounces each
½ pound fresh figs, cut in half
¼ cup grenadine
1 ounce brandy
1 ounce butter
2 cups demi-glaze
1 cup water
½ cup sugar
Salt and pepper

❖ Duck Magret and Fresh Fig Sauce

This open air French sidewalk café in the heart of fashionable El Paseo is an ideal place to leisurely dine while watching the world go by. True to its name, the interior walls are lined with colorful art on consignment from local artists.

"I grew up in Paris, and enjoyed eating at intimate bistros" says owner Didier Bloch. "I like to serve food that reminds me of those charming little bistros all over France and then add a touch of Mediterranean and contemporary Californian influence to my recipes."

The Duck Magret with Fig Sauce is served crispy on the outside and juicy on the inside. The clumps of fresh figs in the sauce give it an added sweetness without being too heavy.

You'll leave with a feeling, that if only for a moment, you were swept away to a charming sidewalk cafe in Paris.

Method —

Sauce: Make a simple syrup by bringing water to a boil, and dissolving the sugar into the boiling water. Once the sugar is dissolved completely, reduce heat, add grenadine and brandy. Let syrup reduce by ⅓. Add figs, cover and cook for 10 minutes over a low fire. Add demi-glaze, salt and pepper. Simmer for 4 minutes, covered. Whisk in butter.

Duck: Preheat oven to 350°F. In a very hot pan, place the magrets skin-side down until the skin is brown, approximately 3 minutes. Turn the duck and put in the oven for 5 minutes. Remove from the oven and slice very thin. Put sauce on plate and arrange the magret on top.

Note: By sautéing the meat with the skin on, the fat becomes melted and brings out the best flavor. The dish is best served rare to medium rare, sliced very thin.

Wine & Spirit Pairing —
Pauillac - Bordeaux

Castelli's

Ristorante

Pollo All' Arancio

SERVES 4 - 6

- 1 quart orange juice
- 1 cup lemon juice
- 1 cup brown sugar
- 2 teaspoons of cream sherry
- 2 teaspoons orange honey
- ½ teaspoon garlic, chopped
- ½ teaspoon salt and pepper mix
- 1 tablespoon butter
- 1 tablespoon flour (may substitute with cornstarch)
- 6 chicken breasts, 12 ounces each, charbroiled

Kiwi slices, orange wedges, strawberry slices, fresh seasonal berries, toasted pine nuts, chopped parsley for garnish

If you have experienced real Italian cooking from an authentic Italian neighborhood restaurant, then you will remember the family feeling you get when you walk in the door at Castelli's. "You are greeted by family and served by a friend," says Michael. Castelli's serves generous portions of quality food at reasonable prices just like the good old days.

The signature selection Pollo All' Arancio is a light, refreshing chicken dish with a fruit and sauce topping that is versatile and can also be served with pork, fish, or duck. This dish not only tastes delicious, but the colors and eye appeal are amazing.

At Castelli's, your dining experience will be one to remember. Executive Chef Brian Altman and his staff will expertly prepare any dish on the menu to your specifications creating your own masterpiece. Buono appetito!

Method —

In a saucepan, combine orange and lemon juice with brown sugar, cream sherry, honey, garlic, salt and pepper and bring to boil. In a smaller saucepan under low heat, melt butter and add flour. Stir until smooth, making a roux. Add roux to the juice mixture in small amounts to thicken. Garnish the cooked chicken breast with fresh fruit. Add the orange glaze sauce. Top with pine nuts and fresh berries. Garnish with parsley.

Note: Try your favorite fresh fruit, like bananas or peaches. This sauce is so versatile you can try it with pork fish or duck.

Wine & Spirit Pairing —
Pio Cesare Cortese Di Gavi — Italy or Fontodi Chianti Classico — Italy

Chez Pierre

An Authentic French Bistro

 Hanger Steak & Heirloom Tomatoes

SERVES 4

Steak:
2   pounds hanger steak,
    8 ounces per person
4   heirloom tomatoes,
    1 per person
2   bags of organic mix spring
    lettuce
½   cup quality vinaigrette
4   tablespoons red onion,
    chopped (optional garnish)
Herbs de Provence

Chimichurri Sauce:
½   cup quality red wine vinegar
½   cup extra virgin olive oil
6   cloves garlic, finely chopped
4   medium shallots, finely
    chopped
2   tablespoons fresh oregano,
    finely chopped
2   tablespoons fresh thyme,
    finely chopped
⅓   cup Italian parsley, chopped
1   teaspoon sea salt
2   tablespoons fresh ground
    black pepper
¾   red pepper flakes (optional)

Translated from French, "Chez Pierre" literally means, "at home with Pierre," and nothing is lost in this translation as Chef/Owner Pierre Pelech and his elegant spouse and partner, Esther, have hospitality written all over them.

Pierre has an amazing passion for authentic French bistro food. "I don't believe in just one signature dish, because everything I cook receives the same attention and love," he says. Pierre's Broiled Hanger Steak proves it.

At Eden Rock at the Hotel du Cap D'Antibes, Pierre learned to cook for the rich and famous of the world. At a special State Dinner in Washington, D.C., he cooked for then Soviet leader Mikhail Gorbachev. While none of us in the desert may be as demanding as Gorbachev, if you appreciate uncompromised quality that also represents real value, Chez Pierre will never disappoint.

We recommend dining on the terrace. It's one of the real hidden pleasures of the desert.

Method —

Mix all the sauce ingredients together and set aside for 30 minutes, allowing flavors to develop.

Season the meat with salt & pepper and herbs de Provence. Broil to your taste, careful not to overcook. Let the meat rest for 5 minutes and slice against the grain.

Arrange the thin-sliced tomatoes around a dinner size plate and season with olive oil, vinegar, and salt and pepper. In the middle of the plate, add a handful of mixed greens seasoned with the vinaigrette. Add the sliced meat on top of the salad and the chimichurri sauce on top of the meat.

Wine & Spirit Pairing —
Côte du Rhône or Pinot Noir

Copley's

On Palm Canyon

Fish:
4   onaga filets, 6 ounces each
    (Hawaiian red snapper)
4   pieces pancetta, thinly sliced
¼   cup olive oil
1   tablespoon butter
Ground white pepper

Vegetables:
1   cup oyster mushrooms,
    cleaned
1   cup corn kernels, cooked
16 pieces asparagus, trimmed,
    cooked al dente

Beet Puree:
2   medium red beets, cooked
    whole with skin
1   cinnamon stick
1   star anise
½   teaspoon fennel seeds
3   tablespoons soft goat
    cheese
Kosher salt
Ground white pepper

Roasted Red Pepper Sauce:
1   large red bell pepper
1   tablespoon butter
⅓   white onion, chopped
¼   cup chicken broth
⅓   cup white wine
2   teaspoons roasted garlic
3   tablespoons heavy whipping
    cream
1   tablespoon tomato paste
Dash ground cayenne pepper

❖ Pancetta Wrapped Onaga

At the top of Palm Canyon Drive sits a charming mid-century structure, once owned by Cary Grant, now Copley's On Palm Canyon. Entering through the front gate into the lush garden courtyard, you will find a large center fountain, ambient lighting, and the restaurant's fresh herb gardens. Opt to dine alfresco or inside the quaint dining room.

Co-owners Chef Andrew Manion Copley, his wife Juliana, and Greg Butterfield are the culinary dream team that has created the perfect balance of international influenced American cuisine and attentive service in a warm and relaxed environment. Chef Andrew's featured dish is the Pancetta Wrapped Onaga. "I love using cured meat with this firm meaty fish. The red beet and goat cheese adds earthiness, while the red pepper sauce brings out a subtle sweetness," he says. Copley's is a marvelous spot in the desert to spend an intimate, romantic evening for two, as well as a great evening of superb cuisine shared with friends.

Method —

Beet Puree: Boil water in a medium-size pot, add salt, beets, cinnamon, star anise and fennel and gently simmer for 10-12 minutes or until the beets are cooked. Cool and peel beets and puree in a food processor. In a saucepan over low heat, warm the beets and goat cheese. Season to taste and set aside.

Roasted Red Pepper Sauce: Roast whole red peppers under a broiler, turning frequently until thoroughly charred. Place the peppers in a food storage bag to steam and loosen the skin. Melt the butter in a saucepan over medium heat. Add the onions and sauté for 3 minutes. Peel the peppers, remove seeds, chop and add to the onions. Increase the heat to high and add chicken broth, wine and simmer for 3 minutes. Remove from heat and allow to cool slightly. Place mixture in the food processor and blend with cayenne pepper and garlic. Strain into a saucepan and add the cream and tomato paste. Whisk thoroughly.

Fish: Preheat oven to 325°F. Season the fish with white pepper. Wrap each piece with one slice of pancetta. In a large sauté pan over medium heat, add half the olive oil. Sear the fish on both sides and place the sauté pan in the oven and cook for 5-6 minutes. Place the beet puree in the center of the plate with the warmed asparagus, corn and mushrooms. Place the onaga on top and drizzle with the red pepper sauce. This dish works well with salmon, halibut or seabass.

Wine & Spirit Pairing —
Old world style wine such as a French Burgundy (red or white)
or a dry Riesling

Cunard's Sandbar

❖ Shrimp "Billye"

16 jumbo shrimp, (6 to 8 count) cleaned and deveined
16 strips pancetta, thinly sliced
16 wooden skewers

Sauce:
2 ½ cups heavy cream
4 tablespoons drained sun-dried tomatoes, (packed in oil) patted dry
2 tablespoons butter

Pasta:
1 pound cooked linguine
¼ cup extra virgin olive oil
¼ cup fresh lemon juice
¼ cup fresh grated parmesan cheese
2 tablespoons fresh thyme
Salt and pepper

For over a quarter century, Bob Cunard's Sandbar Restaurant has proven to be a favorite with visitors, celebrities, and spirited desert locals. With his warm friendly greeting, Bob and his staff of many years welcome you to a delightful evening of good food and friendly service.

The piano bar is such a lively area that many guests opt to remain there for dinner. Some prefer moving into the more secluded wine room, while those who enjoy an intimate dining experience migrate to the outdoor patio area with tiny white lights, moonlit nights, and a warm New Mexico-style adobe fireplace.

This wildly popular eatery offers diverse selections from prime New York steaks, sautéed sole, roasted duck, buttermilk battered fried chicken, fresh fish and nightly specials. Bob has selected to feature their popular Shrimp "Billye." "This dish was created for and named after one of our wonderful guests," notes Cunard.

Method —
Soak skewers in cold water for 1 hour.

Sauce: Julienne the sun-dried tomatoes and combine with cream in a saucepan. Over a medium-high heat, simmer to reduce by half, until a sauce consistency about 10 minutes. Add butter and stir until melted and salt and pepper to taste. Cover and keep warm.

Pasta: Cook according to package instructions. Drain and toss with olive oil, lemon juice, thyme and parmesan cheese, salt and pepper to taste.

Shrimp: Wrap with pancetta, threading 1 shrimp onto each skewer so the shrimp lie flat. Grill or pan-fry shrimps, 3 minutes on each side or until pink and just firm, and pancetta is crisp.

Plating: Remove shrimp from skewer; serve over sauce with pasta and fresh seasonal vegetables.

Wine & Spirit Pairing —
Start with a Kettle One Shaken-Up-Chilled. Bernardus Chardonnay with the shrimp.

Robert Cunard

Exquisite Desserts

Lemon Curd Tart with Raspberries

SERVES 8

Lemon Curd:
3   large eggs
½   cup lemon juice
¾   cup sugar
4   tablespoons sweet butter

Pate Sucre:
¾   cups sugar
3 ½   sticks unsalted butter
1   egg
1   teaspoon vanilla extract
2 ¼   cups bread flour

Tuille Garnish:
½   cup melted butter
½   cup egg white
½   cup sugar
½   cup all purpose flour

Are you looking for that perfectly exquisite dessert to serve at the end of special dinner parties in your home? Look no further. Samantha Ward, Pastry Chef/Owner of Exquisite Desserts is the lady to call. This exclusive boutique bakery specializes in custom designed desserts from scratch. "We work closely with the finest professional chefs in the desert, and a select private clientele, to create and customize every detail for their specific needs. From elaborately decorated wedding cakes to individual desserts with custom designs, we give our utmost attention to detail in creating a remarkable looking and wonderful tasting pieces of art," says Samantha. Because she specializes in custom creations, you will need to call and make an appointment. This ensures that your unique and individualized needs will be met. However, tonight you can serve your guests her fabulous Lemon Curd Tart.

Method —

Lemon Curd: Whisk eggs in a medium size stainless steel bowl. In a saucepan, bring lemon juice, sugar and butter to a boil. Temper the hot lemon juice mixture into the eggs and place bowl on a water bath, with water that is just simmering. Whisk frequently as mixture starts to thicken to prevent eggs from over cooking. Once lemon curd is thickened, take it off water bath and cool.

Pate Sucre: Cream sugar and butter together in a mixer with paddle attachment. Add eggs and vanilla and mix till incorporated. Add the flour and mix only until the dough is smooth. Place dough on a sheet pan and press out as flat as possible to chill down quickly. Cover and refrigerate until dough is firm, about 1 hour. Take ⅓ of dough out at a time. Work on a floured surface and roll dough to approximately ⅛" thickness. Using a fluted cutter, cut circles out and line in mini-muffin tins. (Can be purchased at most home shopping stores). Dough makes approximately 45 mini-tartlets or eight 4" individual tart shells. Bake lined shells in 325°F oven for 10 to 12 minutes, until tart shells have a nice golden color.

Assembly: Once tart shells and lemon curd are cool, pipe lemon curd into tart shells with a pastry bag using a star tip. Garnish with fresh raspberry and a quenelle of crème fraîche.

Tuille Garnish: Mix all ingredients together. Using a firm template spread tuille batter on silicone baking mat. Sprinkle with chopped pistachios (optional). Bake at 325°F for approximately 10 to 12 minutes until tuille is pale golden. Shape immediately while still warm.

Wine & Spirit Pairing
Schramsberg Blanc de Noir Champagne or Inniskillin Icewine

The Falls

Prime Steakhouse & Martini Bar

◈ Ahi Tartar Tower

Wakame salad:

2	cups julienne cucumber, remove seeds
1	cup carrots, julienne
1	tablespoon sweet soy sauce
1	tablespoon chili oil
½	teaspoon sesame oil

Wasabi Crème Fraîche:

½	cup heavy cream
½	cup sour cream
½	teaspoon lemon juice
1	tablespoon hydrated wasabi

Tartar:

¾	pound marinated ahi, diced, sashimi grade
2	ounces sweet chili sauce
2	ounces sweet soy sauce
2	each avocado, diced
⅛	cup Wakame cucumber salad
4	ounces spiral cut carrot
4	ounces pickled ginger
4	ounces wasabi crème fraîche
1	teaspoon black & white sesame seeds

If you're looking for a spectacular dining experience, look no further than The Falls. This contemporary American steakhouse features prime mid-western beef, American Kobe, and fresh seasonal seafood as well as a variety of classics, such as escargot and Caesar salad served table side. "We use locally grown produce, as well as a variety of organic and natural products," says Michael.

Chef Christopher Pope and managing partner Michael Estrada present their Ahi Tartar Tower.

The Palm Springs second-floor location places you at the center of world-famous Palm Canyon Drive. Or dine at the La Quinta location for a truly unique dining experience.

Don't forget to try a famous smokin' martini, in one of the restaurant's exceptional open-air bars. For a special night out with friends, visit The Falls. It's lively. It's hip. It's colorful. It's pure Falls.

Method —

Wakame salad: Combine ingredients and mix thoroughly.

Wasabi Crème Fraîche: Combine ingredients and mix thoroughly.

Tartar: Marinate ahi with the sweet chili and soy sauce, just enough to coat the diced ahi.

Using a ring mold, layer ahi, Wakame salad and diced avocado, lightly pushing all the way down until firm. Before removing ring mold, place spiral cut carrots and ginger on top. Carefully remove ring mold. Once mold is removed, garnish with the wasabi crème fraîche and sesame seeds.

Note: Ring mold is approximately 3-inch in diameter. Tap lightly once all ingredients are layered in the ring mold before removing.

Wine & Spirit Pairing —
Montes "Cherub" Rosé of Syrah or Country Thyme Lemonade Martini

Firecliff

Contemporary California Cuisine

Fish:
4 skinless monkfish tails, 7 ounces each
Cilantro garnish

Hoisin Ginger Sauce:
1 cup Hoisin sauce
1 tablespoon garlic, minced
2 tablespoons ginger, minced
¼ cup fresh lime juice
¼ cup canola oil
¼ cup soy sauce

Noodle Cake:
½ pounds angel hair pasta
4 scallions, sliced diagonally
½ red pepper, cut matchstick size
½ cup bean sprouts

 ## Monkfish on Crispy Noodle Cake

Chef/Owner Patricia Hook has created a dining experience that puts you in "A New York State of Mind With An El Paseo Address." Located on El Paseo, the Rodeo Drive of the desert, Firecliff's open-air dining room and terraces overlook the beautiful landscaped parkway.

Patricia is a highly esteemed chef in the valley who enjoys taking a traditional dish and creating her own unique presentation. Her Monkfish on Crispy Noodle Cake is a perfect example. "This is one of my favorite fish to prepare. Many guests return to enjoy it time and time again due to the wonderful fresh flavors and colorful presentation," says Patricia. The menu is a fine blend of contemporary California cuisine offering the likes of Tea-Smoked Duck Breast, Rack of Colorado Lamb and an outrageously fetching Cinnamon Raisin Bread Pudding with Jack Daniels Crème Anglaise.

Firecliff provides the perfect setting to dine and talk with friends, while enjoying live piano music in the background.

Method —

Hoisin Ginger Sauce: Heat in a medium sauté pan over medium heat, ¼ cup canola oil, garlic and ginger and sauté about 2 minutes. Add Hoisin sauce, stirring about 3 minutes. Add lime juice and soy sauce, heat thoroughly.

Noodle Cake: Cook pasta according to package directions. Drain and set aside. Heat canola oil over medium-high heat in large skillet, add a nest of pasta by turning center of the pasta with tongs. Add to the top center of the noodle cake, scallions, bean sprouts and red peppers. After edge of cake starts to brown continue to cook another 6 to 7 minutes before turning with spatula. Allow to cook for another 5 minutes on the reverse side until brown and crispy. Remove and hold on heated plate.

Monkfish: Pre-heat oven to 400°F. In a large oven proof sauté pan, heat ¼ cup canola oil over medium high heat. Season fish with salt and pepper. Add the monkfish and cook, turning after browned. Cook 3 to 4 minutes on reverse side until brown. Drain oil from sauté pan and drizzle sauce over fish. Place sauté pan in oven for 3 to 4 minutes to glaze fillets.

Plating: Set out 4 plates, place noodle cake onto plate, top with glazed filet, and garnish with cilantro.

Note: Jasmine rice can be substituted for pasta.

Wine & Spirit Pairing —
2006 Grgich Hills Fume Blanc

Patricia Eisele-Hook

Fusion One 11

Martini and Tapas Restaurant

◈ Roasted Breast of Duckling

SERVES 4

Duck:
4 duck breasts, 5 ounces each,
   skin trimmed and scored

Sauce:
3 cups dried cherries
1 cup brown sugar
3 cups chicken stock
¼ cup whole grain mustard
¼ cup olive oil
1 shallot, chopped
1 tablespoon garlic, chopped
Salt and pepper to taste
Blackberries and scallions for
(optional garnish)

Fusion One 11 inhabits an inconspicuous storefront off the northern frontage road of Highway 111. The cosmopolitan décor exudes understated elegance via soft draperies in shades of blue contrasted by electric blue sofa seating. First things first, settle into one of the steel backed bar stools with martini glass cutouts and enjoy one of the best martinis in the desert. Already a local favorite, the bar has name plaques for some of its regulars.

Brothers Scott and Rob Wilson have successfully delivered the tapas inspired concept of small plate dining to the desert. "Many of the items on the menu are substantial enough to serve as entrees, but we suggest ordering several different plates and sharing everything among your dinner companions," say the Wilsons.

Every dish is artfully presented with vibrant color and flavors. Scott and Rob have selected their Roasted Breast of Duckling with garlic mashed potatoes, wild cherry and whole grain mustard reduction as an excellent example. You will enjoy this innovative dining experience.

Method —

Sauce: In a medium saucepan with ⅛ cup of olive oil, sauté shallots, cherries and garlic until translucent. Caramelize the ingredients with brown sugar. Simmer for 5 minutes until adding chicken stock. On low heat, bring to rapid boil. With a quick stick or a blender, puree and strain ingredients.

Duck: Reduce your oven to 375°F. Use remaining olive oil and a non stick sauté pan and sear duck breast skin side down until it is browned. Turn over and finish in the oven until internal temperature reaches 130°F.

Plating: Set out 4 large plates and mound roasted garlic mashed potatoes or starch of your choice in the center of the plate. Ladle 3 to 4 ounces of sauce around starch. Remove the skin and slice breasts on bias into 3 pieces and fan on top of starch. Garnish plate with berries and scallions.

Note: Use caution when placing hot liquids in a blender. Blend small amounts at a time, as the hot liquids tend to expand during blending and can leak out of the container.

Wine & Spirit Pairing —
Opolo Vineyards Zinfandel of Paso Robles

Guillermo's
Restaurante

Shrimp:
3   pounds jumbo Mexican shrimp, cleaned and deveined
3   tablespoons margarine or butter
6   ounces fresh mushrooms, sliced
1   stalk celery, chopped
Salt and pepper

Sauce:
4   cups sour cream
1   cup mayonnaise
2   tablespoons Knorr chicken seasoning mix
2   tablespoons chipotle pepper

Rice:
2   cups white rice
1   cup carrots, finely diced
1   cup corn
1   cup green peas
Cilantro for garnish

 ## Camarones a la Calafia

Here we find authentic Mexican cuisine coupled with a festive atmosphere. In the truest sense, Owner/Chef Guillermo successfully orchestrates every detail while keeping it all in the family! His wife Bertha makes their homemade tamales and a terrific Mexican flan. All five of their children, as well as nieces and nephews, are actively involved on a daily basis.

The restaurant prides itself on having one of the finest collections (300+ bottles) of premium tequilas in the desert. But nothing overshadows the wonderful cuisine where much care is given to the conceptualization and preparation of every dish. Guillermo embraces a style of urban & coastal Mexico dishes, saying "I look to bring traditional ingredients, with a combination of flavor, a hint of spice and simplicity of presentation." He shares this approach in a favorite sautéed shrimp dish.

If you love authentic Mexican food and enjoy casual dining, Guillermo's family is waiting to exceed your expectations.

Method —

Rice: Prepare rice according to package. In a small pan of boiling water, blanch corn, peas and carrots. Set aside. When rice is cooked, mix corn, peas and carrots together.

Sauce: In a saucepan over low heat, mix together sour cream, mayonnaise and Knorr seasoning. Add chipotle pepper to taste to taste. Less for mild, more for spicy. Continue to stir until mixture is creamy. Keep warm on low heat, add sautéed celery and mushrooms (see below).

Shrimp: In a sauté pan over medium-high heat, add margarine or butter, chopped celery and mushrooms. Cook 5 to 7 minutes. Remove celery and mushrooms and add to sauce. Season shrimp with salt and pepper using the same sauté pan. Add shrimp and cook 5 to 7 minutes, adding more margarine if necessary.

Plating: Spoon rice into a cup and press firmly to form. Position a plate over the top of the cup and invert rice onto plate. Spoon sauce around rice and add shrimp. Top with cilantro.

Note: Sauce can be prepared ahead and stored in refrigerator for up to seven days. Warm on a low heat before serving.

Wine & Spirit Pairing —
La Crema Chardonnay

Le Basil

Southeast Asian Cuisine

✦ Thai Chicken Satay

SERVES **6 - 12 SKEWERS**

Satay:
- 1 pound boneless, skinless chicken breast
- ½ cup canned coconut milk
- ½ cup condensed milk
- 1 tablespoon vegetable oil
- 3 tablespoons brown sugar
- 1 teaspoon Indian yellow curry powder
- ¼ teaspoon sea salt
- 1 tablespoon fish sauce
- 12 wooden bamboo skewers, soaked in water for 30 minutes

Peanut Sauce:
- 1 19 ounce can coconut milk
- 2 tablespoons Musmun curry paste or red curry paste
- 5 tablespoons sugar
- ½ teaspoon salt
- 1 tablespoon tamarind sour soup base mix from Thailand
- 3 tablespoons natural chunky peanut butter or ground peanuts (no salt)

Thai Cucumber Relish:
- 3 tablespoons rice vinegar
- 2 tablespoons water
- 1 tablespoon sugar
- 1 cucumber, cut into quarter lengthwise, then cut across into thin slices
- 2 shallots, chopped
- 1 red Thai Chili finely chopped (optional to make it spicy)

In a labor of love, husband and wife team Orn and Chef Tom Chotiyanonta work together in perfect harmony delivering fresh Thai and Vietnamese dishes with a French twist. "We are delighted to open our doors and welcome our many new wonderful friends, here in the desert, to dine with us," says the couple.

With flavors so fresh, you can taste each component. Many of the ingredients used are imported directly from Thailand. The menu offers an appealing list of fresh, light dishes layered with contrasting flavors and textures. Selections range from enticing appetizers, soups and salads to entrées that include beef, chicken, duck, pork and fresh seafood preparations. Lemon grass, basil, chili sauce, coconut, pineapple and peanuts are some of the flavorful ingredients that are worked skillfully into the various dishes. Beverages include a good selection of imported and domestic beers as well as a well-chosen wine list.

Method —

Chicken: Slice chicken into strips ¼ inches thick and 2 inches wide. Combine all other ingredients. Place chicken in mixture and turn to coat well. Place in refrigerator to marinate for at least 2 hours. (Overnight is preferable). To cook, thread chicken strips onto bamboo skewers and grill over charcoal on fairly high heat. Turn them regularly and brush liberally with remaining marinade until crispy outside, but moist inside. It should take about 5 minutes to cook them well.

Peanut Sauce: Combine coconut milk, curry paste, sugar, salt, tamarind soup base mix and peanut butter in a saucepan. Cook over moderate heat just until mixture boils, stirring constantly to break up curry paste and peanut butter. Mix well. Remove from heat and stir until smooth.

Thai Cucumber Relish: Mix vinegar, sugar and salt together and simmer over medium heat until dissolved and sauce slightly thickens. Remove from the heat and allow the mixture to cool down. Just before serving, pour the cold sauce over the vegetables.

Note: You may also use the same recipe with beef, pork, or large prawns. Soy sauce may be used as a substitute for the fish sauce. You may also use this peanut sauce recipe for peanut salad dressing by adding water (about 3 tablespoons) and stirring while peanut sauce mixture is still warm.

Wine & Spirit Pairing —
2005 Jekel Monterey Riesling

Lord Fletcher Inn

✦ Braised Short Ribs

SERVES 6

Ribs:
6   short ribs
3 ½ cups beef broth
¼   cup onion, chopped
2   bay leaves

Sauce:
¼   cup onion, chopped
½   teaspoon thyme
½   cup burgundy wine
¼   cup margarine
4   tablespoons flour
Salt and pepper
Kitchen Bouquet

Over 40 years ago, Ron Fletcher made his vision of creating a true English country inn in the desert a reality. Carrying on the family tradition, Lord Fletcher's is currently operated by Ron's son Michael.

The authentic atmosphere of dining in an English country inn is enhanced by an extensive collection of antiques and historic prints. But, it is the traditional food and caring staff that bring it all to life.

Michael offered great insight into the history of their selected recipe. "Our original chef from England developed our signature dish unlike any other," he said. "We specify a custom cut piece of meat and marry it to our Bordelaise sauce. It has been on our menu since we opened our doors, and remains very popular to this day."

You are sure to enjoy this entertaining at home. But, you will have to go to Lord Fletcher's if you want their special 20-ounce custom cut.

Method —

Short Ribs: Pre-heat oven to 550°F, place ribs in roasting pan and brown in a hot oven for about 20 minutes. Add beef broth, bay leaves, onion and water to just cover ribs. Lower temperature to 450°F. Cover and cook until tender, about 2 hours. Keeping ribs warm, prepare sauce with remaining stock.

Sauce: Skim excess fat from stock. In a saucepan bring stock to a boil, add onions and thyme, and simmer for 20 minutes. Add burgundy and simmer 5 minutes more. In another small saucepan over low heat, melt margarine. Stirring constantly, add flour until (roux) mixture is well blended and slightly browned. Gradually add roux to stock, stirring constantly until desired thickness. Salt and pepper to taste. For dark brown color, add a few drops of Kitchen Bouquet. Strain sauce through a fine sieve or cheese cloth. Pour over ribs and serve.

Note: Ask the butcher for the largest cut of short ribs. We serve our short ribs with Yukon gold potatoes and sweet and sour red cabbage.

Wine and Spirit Paring —
Foley Pinot Nior

Los Pepes

Mexican Grill

2   pounds tri-tip beef,
     cut into strips
½   cup garlic cloves,
     finely chopped
1   tablespoon all-purpose flour
6   roasted poblano peppers
3   roasted jalapeños
1   pound roasted tomatoes
2   tablespoons chicken base
2   tablespoons extra virgin
     olive oil
2   teaspoons salt
1 ½ cups water
Pepper to taste

 ## Caldillo Durangeño Beef Stew

Pepe and Silvia invite you to sample their family recipes and the ambiance of their authentic Northern Mexican décor. At Los Pepes, the customer comes first. The personal service and comfortable surroundings will bring you back time and again.

A family owned and operated restaurant, Los Pepes offers a variety of fresh dishes which trace their roots to the Mexican States of Durango and Michoacan. "It is with great joy we bring a little bit of our home town here to Palm Desert," says the couple.

Pepe has selected their Caldillo Durangeño Beef Stew. It's simple, prepared with care, and it's delicious! In addition to the traditional ethnic recipes, the owners have added dishes to the menu which were discovered from their travels in California and abroad.

Los Pepes offers a full-service bar, featuring their renowned margaritas.

Method —

Cut the peppers into strips (reserve 2 peppers sliced for garnish) and dice the tomatoes. Heat the oil in a medium pan. Add the beef strips, onion, and garlic, stirring over medium heat until the beef is browned. Add the salt, tomatoes and peppers. Cook uncovered over medium heat about 4 minutes. Add the water and the chicken base. Dissolve the flour with 3 tablespoons of water in a dish then add to the stew. Continue cooking until the meat is tender and the stew thickens, about 8 minutes. Garnish with remaining sliced peppers and top with cilantro.

Roasting Tomatoes: Heat 1 teaspoon of oil in a saucepan. Add tomatoes and grill until the skin is lightly charred. Remove from pan and set aside. Remove the skin with your hands.

Roasting Peppers: Place the peppers over the medium flame of a gas stove. Turn the peppers until their skin is lightly charred. Place the peppers in a bag and close. Set aside for 10 minutes. Remove the skin with your hands. Cut the top of the pepper by the stem and remove. Cut pepper in half. Remove the membranes and seeds. Cut into strips.

Note: The roasting process makes it easier to remove the skin.

Wine & Spirit Pairing —
Dos Equis XX Amber beer or your favorite margarita

pepe and Silvia

Matchbox

Vintage Pizza Bistro

❖ Grilled Citrus Scallops

16   large diver scallops

Marinade:
1   cup extra virgin olive oil
1   cup soy sauce
3   tablespoons brown sugar
2   tablespoons coarse ground black pepper
2   tablespoons garlic, chopped
1   tablespoon parsley, chopped

Sesame Sticky Rice:
3   cups Japanese style sticky rice
5   cups water
½   cup soy sauce
¾   cup sesame oil
2   tablespoons mixed sesame seeds
1   tablespoon dried parsley

Citrus Soy Sauce:
1   lemon
1   lime
1   orange
½   medium yellow onion
1   stalk celery, leaves included
2   quarts water
1 ½   cups soy sauce
1 ½   cups granulated sugar
½   cup cornstarch
½   cup water
Julienned carrot , ginger and chives for garnish

Matchbox Vintage Pizza Bistro is an exciting restaurant with a decidedly hip and urban feel. *Voted Best Pizza in the Valley*, Matchbox serves made-to-order fresh pizza baked in a wood fired oven.

The menu is equally divided into two parts. The first features incomparable East Coast-style thin crust pizza. The second includes chef-driven bistro fare featuring fresh fish, steak, chops, innovative salads and sandwiches. Chef Christopher Pope selected one of his favorites — Grilled Citrus Marinated Scallops.

Dine in the main dining room, at either of the two bars, al fresco on one of several balconies, or pull up a chair in front of the fire pit. Both overlook Palm Canyon Drive in the heart of Palm Springs. A local favorite spot for happy hour, enjoy the award-winning mini burgers topped with onion straws and the refreshing drink specials. Matchbox Vintage Pizza Bistro is open nightly.

Method —

Scallops: Over medium to high heat in non-stick skillet, sear scallops approximately 2-3 minutes on each side. Place sticky rice in center of serving plate. Un-mold and arrange seared scallops around rice. Drizzle citrus soy sauce around and on scallops, garnish with toasted mixed sesame seeds, chopped chives, and pickled ginger.

Marinade: Combine first 6 ingredients and mix well. Place scallops in container, pour marinade over scallops, cover and refrigerate for at least two hours. Overnight will give the best flavor.

Sesame Sticky Rice: In medium saucepan, combine rice and water. Bring to a boil and cook for 15 minutes over medium heat. Turn off heat and cover, allowing the water to finish absorbing. When all the water is absorbed, add remaining ingredients. Mold rice into whatever shape or serving size you like.

Citrus Soy Sauce: Combine water, celery, rind and the juices of lemon, lime and orange in medium saucepan. Bring to a simmer for 40 minutes and strain. Place back on medium heat and add soy and sugar. Simmer for 30 minutes. Thicken with cornstarch and water. (Mix cornstarch and water ahead of time till smooth)

Wine & Spirit Pairing —
Chimay Belgium Beer or Matchbook Chardonnay

McGowan's
Irish Inn

4   lamb shanks
2   tablespoons extra virgin
    olive oil
1   large raw onion, chopped
2   raw carrots, chopped
2   raw green peppers,
    chopped
1   14 ounce can of peeled
    tomatoes
2   tablespoons tomato paste
½   cup dry vermouth
2   tablespoons flour
2   cups water
Salt and pepper to taste

❖ Lamb Shank

It's been said that there are two types of people-those that are Irish and those that wish to be Irish. McGowan's Irish Inn, the only Irish restaurant in the desert, will bring a smile to your face with its inviting atmosphere, friendly crowd, and authentic Irish comfort food.

Mary McGowan shares the recipe for Lamb Shank, the house specialty for 19 years, because it was a family favorite. Her parents were from Ireland and the menu features the same dishes that her mother served at home.

There is something for everyone from soups, pasta, corned beef and cabbage, chicken and dumplings, meat loaf, prime rib and the fish of the day. Desserts include bread pudding with vanilla ice cream and homemade cheesecake.

Mary tells us, "The best compliment that I can receive is when our guests come back and bring their friends and family." Mary's Irish eyes are always smiling at McGowan's.

Method —

Pre-heat oven to 350°F. Place lamb shanks on baking sheet and put into the oven for ½ hour. Remove the lamb shank and place into a deep roasting pan. Add onions, carrots, peppers and tomatoes. In a separate bowl, combine tomato paste, dry vermouth, flour and salt and pepper. Whisk together. Pour over vegetables and lamb shanks. Add enough water to cover the meat. Seal roasting pan with aluminum foil. Return to oven and bake for one hour or until fork goes into lamb easily. Serve with mint jelly.

Note: For that true Irish meal, serve with mash potatoes and peas. As for dessert, you can't go wrong with bread pudding, served hot and topped with vanilla ice cream.

Wine & Sprit Pairing —
Sonoma-Cutrer Les Pierres, Murphy Goode Cabernet Sauvignon or Guinness Beer

Mary McGowan

The Nest

Stuffed Cannelloni

Crepes:
- 2 eggs
- ⅔ cup milk
- 1 tablespoon butter, melted
- ½ cup all-purpose flour
- ¼ teaspoon salt

Meat Filling:
- ¾ pound ground veal
- ½ pound ground chicken
- 2 tablespoons butter
- 1 tablespoon minced fresh parsley
- ½ cup grated parmesan cheese
- ½ teaspoon salt
- 1 dash ground black pepper
- 1 dash ground nutmeg

White Sauce:
- 2 tablespoons butter
- 2 tablespoons all-purpose flour
- 1 cup milk
- ¼ teaspoon salt
- ⅛ teaspoon ground black pepper
- ⅛ teaspoon ground nutmeg
- 2 cups tomato pasta sauce (homemade or your favorite jar sauce)
- 2 cups shredded mozzarella cheese
- ¾ cup grated parmesan cheese

Calling the desert home for more than 40 years, The Nest is a favorite of the country club set, as a legendary late nightspot with a lively piano bar and energetic dance floor. Frequent celebrity drop-ins are often invited to perform at the piano with Tim Burleson.

For the past 28 years, June and Ted Hane have been your hosts. "We have one of the lowest turnover rates for staffing in the valley. This insures consistency, professionalism, and recognition when you come back to visit," says June.

The menu offers diversity with several Swiss touches, French entrees, and a few Italian dishes to make things more interesting. Ted is Swiss, the chef Michel Schenker is French, and the Italian food is just along for the fun! We like the house specialty of stuffed cannelloni. An evening at The Nest is just what is needed after a great day of enjoying the desert.

Method —

Crepes: In a medium bowl beat eggs thoroughly, then add milk and butter. Beat in flour and salt until smooth. Brown crepes in a medium hot skillet, making them 6 to 8 inches in circumference, set aside.

Meat Filling: Brown veal and chicken in butter in a large skillet over medium high heat. Stir in the parsley, cheese, salt, pepper and nutmeg. Let cool.

White Sauce: In a small saucepan over medium heat, cook flour and butter together for 1 minute. Stir in salt, pepper and nutmeg, then stir in milk and continue to cook until thick. Spread half of the tomato pasta sauce in the bottom of a 9 x 13 inch baking dish. Spoon the meat mixture into prepared crepes, folding over all sides of crepe to form palm-sized bundles, place filled crepes, seam side down, in baking dish. Cover with remaining tomato pasta sauce and pour white sauce over all. Cover with mozzarella cheese and top with Parmesan cheese. Bake in the pre-heated 375°F oven for 20 to 30 minutes, or until cheese is bubbly and brown around the edges. Serve hot with crusty garlic bread.

Note: Crepe batter is best if left to set for half an hour before using.

Wine and Spirit Pairing —
Pinot Grigio or Chardonnay

Paseo Palms
Bar and Grill

4 slices cinnamon swirl bread, or bread of your choice 1 ½ inches thick

Dipping Batter:
3 eggs, beaten
½ cup cream
¼ cup orange juice
1 tablespoon honey
½ teaspoon vanilla, optional
½ teaspoon cinnamon
4 slices bread

Orange Crème Anglaise:
2 cups half-and-half
1 teaspoon orange zest, freshly grated
6 large egg yolks
½ cup granulated sugar
2 tablespoons Grand Marnier, or other orange-flavored liqueur
1 teaspoon vanilla extract

Macadamia Brittle recipe:
2 7 ounce jars macadamia nuts
2 cups granulated sugar
½ cup light corn syrup
2 tablespoons butter
½ teaspoon baking soda

❖ Orange Brûléed French Toast

A distinctive positive vibe is going on at the corner of Hwy 74 and El Paseo! Inside high ceilings, cool artwork, and black & white striped cabanas strike a dramatic Hollywood set atmosphere. Outside, there is a subtle pulse of Palm Beach where superlative dining al fresco reigns supreme on the front terrace or the courtyard patio off the Cabana Bar. From the extensive array of amazing dishes, Executive Chef Eldon Pico, a graduate of the California Culinary Academy, has selected his unique Orange Brûléed French Toast. Owners Mitch Harper and Kathy Maddox note, "If the preparation of this dish seems a bit exhausting, we suggest that you relax and let us do the work for you. You deserve it."

Method —

Dipping Batter: In a large bowl, mix beaten eggs with the cream, orange juice, honey, vanilla and cinnamon. Dip a slice of bread into mixture then place on a heated griddle that has been sprayed with nonstick cooking spray. Cook for 1-2 minutes on each side on medium-high heat or until desired doneness. Cut slices in half (one slice per person) and place on the plate. Top with anglaise, then macadamia brittle. Top with orange segments, dust with powdered sugar, garnish with mint sprigs.

Orange Crème Anglaise: In a medium saucepan, bring the half-and-half, ¼ cup of sugar and orange zest to a simmer over medium-high heat. Remove from the heat. In a medium bowl, whisk together the egg yolks and remaining ¼ cup sugar until thick, about 3 minutes. Gradually whisk in about ¾ cup of the hot half-and-half, mixing well. Add the egg mixture to the saucepan with the remaining half-and-half. Cook, stirring over medium heat, until it thickens, about 5 minutes. Remove from heat and place saucepan in a large bowl of ice water to chill mixture quickly. Add the Grand Marnier and vanilla, stir to combine. Cover with plastic wrap, pressing down on the surface to prevent a skin from forming. Refrigerate until completely cool, about 2 hours or overnight.

Macadamia Brittle: Butter a large baking sheet and set aside. Cut nuts in half and set aside.

In a 10-inch nonstick skillet, combine sugar with ½ cup water and corn syrup. Cook over medium-high heat, stirring occasionally, until golden brown. Stir in nuts. Cook, stirring constantly, until medium brown (do not burn). Remove from heat. Quickly stir in butter and baking soda. Pour onto prepared baking sheet. Cool on pan on wire rack. Break into pieces. Makes about 2 ½ cups.

Wine and Spirit Paring
Mimosa or Champagne

Piero's Acqua Pazza

California Bistro

 ## Salmon en Papillote

Salmon:
4   9 ounce pieces wild salmon
1   pound fresh spinach
1   cup fennel bulb
12 petite red potatoes
1   cup cherry tomatoes
4   teaspoons oregano, freshly
    chopped
4   pieces parchment paper
Pinch of salt and pepper
Drizzle olive oil

Champagne Beurre Blanc:
⅓   cup champagne vinegar
⅓   cup dry white wine
2   shallots, finely chopped
½   lemon, juiced
2   bay leaves
½   cup heavy cream
½   pound unsalted butter,
    cubed
2   tablespoons chopped chives
Salt and pepper

Here we have the best of both worlds. Dine indoors and enjoy an exciting California bistro atmosphere with gentle water features throughout. Or, dine al fresco and enjoy great mountain views from the lovely riverside terrace, where live music is offered daily. In either case, the combination of food, service and ambiance creates a memorable dining experience.

Restaurateur Piero Pierattoni shares, "We combine high quality, fresh ingredients with our passion for savory foods along with a dash of innovation from Executive Chef Arturo Cassillas and his dedicated staff."

The menu is extensive and diverse, offering wonderful salads, gourmet pizzas, pastas, steaks and more. Chef Arturo selected to feature their Fresh Salmon in Parchment recipe. Here is a wonderfully flavorful dish, presented with a real flair that dinner guests in your home would only expect to see in a fine restaurant such as Piero's Acqua Pazza. As if by magic, here it is from their kitchen to yours!

Method —

Salmon: Halve fennel bulb lengthwise. Remove most of core, leaving enough intact to keep layers together when sliced. Blanch fresh spinach, fennel and red potatoes. Set aside. Cut individual pieces of parchment paper the size of a half cookie sheet. Lay out the parchment paper individually and drizzle a small amount of olive oil. Place the spinach and fennel on one side of the parchment paper, making a bed for the salmon. Place the salmon on the paper and stack the red potatoes and cherry tomatoes on top. Finish by adding the oregano with a pinch of salt and pepper. Fold the paper into a package and bake in the oven at 375°F for 20 minutes. Serve in paper with the champagne beurre blanc sauce, roasted vegetables and crispy onions.

Champagne Beurre Blanc: In a heavy 2 quart saucepan, combine vinegar, wine, shallots, lemon, and bay leaves to make an infusion. Simmer over medium heat for 5 to 8 minutes until the mixture is reduced to a wet paste, about 2 tablespoons. Add the cream and continue to simmer until reduced again to about 2 tablespoons. Reduce the heat to low and remove the bay leaves. Whisk in the chunks of butter in small batches. The butter should melt without the sauce getting too hot, producing a creamy emulsified sauce. Season with salt and pepper, fold in the chives, and serve immediately. Keep covered in a warm place for a few hours if needed.

Note: Cream is added to make the sauce more stable and less likely to separate.

Wine & Spirit Pairing —

Luna Pinot Grigio from Napa or Fiddlehead Cellars Sauvignon Blanc from Santa Ynez Valley

Purple Palm

Colony Palms Hotel

SERVES 4

Red Pepper Syrup:
3   pounds red peppers, cored and seeded

Cantaloupe-Habanero Tahitian Vanilla Bean Dressing:
¾   large cantaloupe, peeled and sliced
½   habanero chili, stemmed
½   teaspoon vanilla beans
4   ounces extra virgin olive oil
1   tablespoon shallots, minced
Salt and pepper to taste

Sea Bass and Scallop:
4   slices Parma prosciutto, cut in half lengthwise
4   jumbo sea scallops, halved
1   medium purple Peruvian potato
8   Chilean sea bass medallions, ½ ounce each
1   tablespoon olive oil
1   teaspoon sweet chili sauce
½   cup mango, peeled and diced small
½   cup avocado, peeled and diced small
Black pepper to taste

The Purple Palm represents a bold step forward in world class cuisine in the desert. Chef Jim Shiebler prepares Mediterranean inspired dishes using classic French cooking techniques. In addition, Shiebler enhances each dish with a contemporary twist which elevates the food to the level of a Michelin-starred restaurant. Chef Shiebler, calls his recipe for duo of scallops and sea bass, "a yin-yang of hot and cold."

In keeping with the blending of old and new, the setting of the Purple Palm in the lushly landscaped courtyard of The Colony Palms Hotel evokes the glamour of Palm Springs in the 1930s when this historic hotel, featuring magnificent Spanish Colonial architecture, was built. The stunning interiors of the restaurant were designed by Martyn Lawrence-Bullard, named by Architectural Digest as one of the top 100 designers in the world.

Both the food and the ambience perfectly fuse "Classic" and "Hip."

Method —

Red Pepper Syrup: Using a juicer machine, juice the red peppers and place in a saucepan. Bring to a boil and reduce the quantity to a light syrup consistency.

Cantaloupe Dressing: Using a juicer machine, juice the cantaloupe and habanero. Place in a saucepan and reduce until syrup consistency. Add all remaining ingredients. Be careful not to touch inner flesh with your hands.

Sea Bass & Scallop: Season the scallop halves and Chilean sea bass with cracked pepper. Wrap the scallops with the prosciutto and the bass with purple potato slices. Heat olive oil to smoke point. Add seafood and cook until medium rare, golden brown and crispy on all sides. In a bowl, combine chili sauce and mango.

Plating: Place a small 1 ½ inch circular ring mold onto a plate. Fill with diced avocado on one side and mango on the other, and press down gently to form avocado and mango. Drizzle with cantaloupe dressing and red pepper syrup. Alternate the sea bass and scallops on the plate, remove ring and garnish with Italian parsley sprig.

Note: Syrup and dressing can be prepared ahead of time and kept in the refrigerator.

Wine & Spirit Pairing —
Brancott Sauvignon Blanc, Marlborough, New Zealand 2001

Red Tomato

Original House of Lamb

SERVES **6**

Chicken Gravy:
4   2 ½ pound chickens
1   large onion, peeled and
     quartered
4   teaspoons chicken base
¾   cup milk
¾   cup cornstarch
4   drops yellow food coloring
Green peas
Salt and Pepper

Dumplings:
2   cups Bisquick baking mix
⅔   cup milk
Makes 10–12 dumplings

A little bit of Hollywood can still be found in the desert. Owner Bill Beck's collection of original antiques and old Hollywood memorabilia lines the walls, and the menu itself spotlights creations such as The Mary Pickford, The Charlie Chaplin and The Liz Taylor. For those who love lamb, the star of the show is the "fall-off-the-bone" Albanian Lamb Shanks that offer a blend of Middle Eastern flavors. Regular guest stars include wonderful Italian dishes and great pizza.

Growing up in a very patriotic family, and serving in the U.S. Navy, Bill has put on the marquee, as the featured attraction, his Grandma's All-American Chicken'n Dumplings recipe. The only thing that could make this dish more American would be a slice of apple pie.

"Here at The Red Tomato, a dining experience encompasses the very finest of food and friendly service that consistently results in our guests returning again and again with great anticipation," says Bill.

Method —

Chicken: Place the chicken and onion in a large soup pot. Add 5 quarts of water and bring to a boil. Simmer until the leg bone pulls off easily, about 45 minutes. Remove the chicken from the pot. When it is cool enough to handle, remove the skin and separate the meat from the bones. After removing the chicken from the broth, pour the broth through a strainer to remove bits of onion. Return the strained broth to the soup pot, add chicken base and food coloring, taste for salt and bring to a back to a boil. In a separate bowl combine cornstarch and enough cold milk to dissolve the cornstarch. Whisk until smooth, slowly add to the chicken stock. Be careful not to make it too thick. It should be the consistency of pancake batter.

Dumplings: Mix the Bisquick and milk until soft dough forms. Place about ½ inch water in a large saucepan, using a vegetable steamer basket placed at the bottom. Coat with non-stick spray to prevent dumplings from sticking. Bring water to a boil. Scoop dumpling batter with a tablespoon, drop dumplings by tablespoons onto basket, (do not allow water to touch dumpling) leaving room in between for expansion. Steam 8 minutes covered. Gently remove dumplings and place in gravy. Serve with blanched green pea and cranberry sauce.

Note: Test dumpling by cutting in half to make sure they are cooked through. If you have questions just call Bill.

Wine & Spirit Pairing —
Pinot Noir

Riccio's

Italian

2   veal shanks, 3 inches in height
8   cups crushed tomatoes
1½ cups red wine
2   tablepoons garlic, crushed
1   carrot, diced
1   onion, diced
1   celery, diced
3   bay leaves
1   bouquet garni of fresh
    thyme, sage and rosemary
Olive oil
Salt and pepper

Risotto:
1   cup Arborio risotto
½ onion, diced
1½ cups white wine
3   cups or more vegetable or
    chicken stock
1   tablespoon unsalted butter
¾ cup grated parmesan cheese
4   tablespoons olive oil
2   tablespoons saffron threads,
    crushed

❖ Osso Buco alla Milanese

For three generations, Riccio's Italian restaurant is revered as "home away from home" to visiting celebrities and loyal locals. Right from the onset, the intimate dining room creates a romantic Old World atmosphere. And, at the end of the evening, the live music from the piano bar will beckon you to enjoy their famous flaming coffee. But, it is the incredible fine dining experience that happens between the two that will compel your returning "home" again and again.

Owner/Chef Danny Riccio confidently prepares wonderful food using nothing but absolutely fresh ingredients. His featured dish, Osso Buco alla Milanese with Risotto Zafferano, comes with simple instructions, "This is a very demanding dish. Take no shortcuts. Do it right. Lots of ingredients and love and slow cooking," he says.

At Riccio's you are not just "out to dinner," but immersed in the art of fine dining. Here, you become part of the family. Welcome home.

Method —

Veal Shank: Pre-heat oven to 350°F. Season the veal shanks with salt and pepper and lightly dust each side with flour. Heat a large Dutch oven over medium-high heat, add the olive oil and brown the veal shanks on all sides. Remove the browned veal shanks to a paper towel lined plate. In the same hot pan, add the onion, celery and carrots and cook the vegetables over a medium high heat until they are transparent, stirring occasionally. As the vegetables are browning, add the garlic and herbs. Add the wine to deglaze the pan and reduce. Place the veal shanks back into the pan, add tomatoes and bring to high heat. Cover. Put in oven for two hours, until the veal shanks are very tender and the meat is falling off the bone.

Risotto: Sauté onion in olive oil and butter over medium-high heat until lightly browned. Add rice and mix with a wooden spoon to coat for about 30 seconds. Add wine and reduce. Add 1 cup of stock and cook, stirring, until absorbed. Repeat with a second cup. As the rice becomes dry, add stock in ½ cup increments, cooking and stirring until it is absorbed. When risotto is tender, add parmesan cheese and finish with saffron.

Note: Check with the butcher for a large cut of the veal shank. Lamb shank can be substituted.

Wine and Spirit Pairing —
Amarone della Valpolicella or Barolo

Riccio's

Steak & Seafood

 ## Mixed Mediterranean Grill

SERVES 2

8   mussels, cleaned
8   clams, cleaned
2   5 ounce wild salmon filets
6   scallops
6   jumbo shrimp
2   cloves fresh garlic, peeled
    and chopped
½   cup white wine
2   lobster tails, 8 ounces each or
    1 whole main lobster, split
1   tenderloin, 6 ounces
    cut into 1-inch cubes
1   yellow bell pepper,
    sliced in 2 by 1-inch pieces
1   red pepper, sliced in 2 by
    1-inch pieces
½   white or yellow onion, sliced
    in 2 by 1-inch pieces
4   cherry tomatoes
⅓   cup extra virgin olive oil
1   teaspoon crushed red
    pepper flakes
Paprika
Lemon wedges
1 bamboo skewer

With this second dining venue, the Riccio brothers, Richard and Danny, proudly carry on their family tradition with the style and consistent quality that has been renowned for decades at their original Riccio's Restaurant. "Our steak and seafood cuisine is an extension of the Riccio style of cooking and dining. We bring Mediterranean flavors, textures, and love of the food to our guests," say the brothers. Riccio's relaxed environment caters to the entire family and offers an amazingly upscale children's menu.

The outside patio on the corner is a perfect vantage point for people watching, while the dining room features intimate booths, warm colors and dark wood accents. The menu lives up to its namesake and is complimented with daily specials inspired by culinary staples and preparation techniques of Mediterranean corridor countries. Our featured dish, The Mixed Grill, is something that can be shared as an appetizer or offered as a dinner entrée.

Method —

Seafood: Discard any mussels or clams with a broken shell or those that do not close when sharply tapped. In a large sauté pan over medium-high heat, sauté 2 tablespoons olive oil, red pepper flakes and garlic and cook until garlic is lightly browned, about 1 minute. Add white wine, mussels and clams. Cover and steam until shells open, reserving juice. Bring a pot of salted water to a boil. Add the lobsters and boil until just cooked through, about 10 to 12 minutes. Drain the lobster and put them in a bowl of ice water to stop the cooking. Drain the lobsters well, and carefully remove the tail meat from the shell. In a medium bowl, mix shrimp, scallops and lobster meat, season with salt, pepper and 2 tablespoons olive oil and set aside. Brush the salmon on all sides with olive oil and season with salt and pepper. Place the fish on a large grill pan and cook for about 2 minutes. Turn the fish and cook for an additional 2 minutes. Add shrimp, scallops and lobster to the grill. Turn the fish over and cook for an additional 2 minutes or until cooked through to the desired degree of doneness.

Meat: Brush tenderloin with olive oil and season generously with salt and pepper. In a small bowl, combine peppers, onion and cherry tomato, 1 teaspoon olive oil, season with salt and pepper. Grill the tenderloin cubes, peppers and onions turning frequently until the meat is rare or medium rare, about 3 to 4 minutes.

Plating: Thread pepper, onion, tomato and tenderloin pieces, alternating as you go, and top with tomato. Place skewer in center of plate and surround with seafood.

Wine and Spirit Pairing —
Jermann Pinot Grigio, Italy

The Right Bank

Pork Chops:
6   bone-in pork chops,
    1 pound each
2   cups chopped hazelnuts
¾   cup flour
2   eggs
3   tablespoons olive oil

Cranberry Chutney:
2   cups fresh cranberries
2   apples, sliced and cored
1   orange, sliced with rind
1   cup brown sugar

Orange Sauce:
2   cups fresh orange juice
1   cup Cointreau
1   cup brown sugar
4   tablespoons cornstarch

❖ Rack of Pork Sunset Strip

The Right Bank offers modern world cuisine. Its elegant, comfortable atmosphere, delicious food and friendly staff welcome diners with the kind of personal service that you expect from a local Valley favorite. Boasting many traditional dishes with modern interpretations, you can choose from such favorites as Escargot, Filet Dionisio, Shrimp Hong Kong, Juan Penne Rigatoni and Rack of Pork Sunset Strip.

"Holidays are very special to us," says Alex. The Right Bank creates a time-honored fare for families on Thanksgiving, Christmas and New Year's Eve. Many couples also enjoy Valentine's Day, Easter Brunch, and Mother's Day.

The Right Bank is open on Sundays for their popular champagne brunch along with dinner nightly. The restaurant has a great wine list and full bar service. In season, enjoy Bill Marx at the piano.

Method —

Cranberry Chutney: Using on/off turns, coarsely chop cranberries, apples and orange slices together in a food processor. Gradually mix in brown sugar.

Orange Sauce: In a saucepan over medium-high heat, combine orange juice, Cointreau and brown sugar. Cook until it comes to a boil for about 10 minutes. Meanwhile, slowly add enough water to dilute the cornstarch, whisk until smooth, and gradually add to sauce until thickened. Reduce heat to low to keep warm.

Pork Chops: In three separate dishes place, flour, eggs (slightly beaten) and chopped hazelnuts. Dredge chops in flour, egg and then hazelnuts. Set a large 12-inch sauté pan over medium-high heat. Add olive oil. Once hot, place the pork chops in the pan. Sear the pork chops about 3 minutes. Turn over and sear on the second side for an additional 3 minutes. Remove chops from pan and place on a baking sheet in a 400°F pre-heated oven. Roast the pork chops until an instant-read thermometer inserted registers 150°F, about 10 to 12 minutes for medium. Remove from the oven. To plate, spoon cranberry chutney on top of pork chop, drizzle with orange sauce, garnish with orange peel and rosemary sprig.

Wine & Spirit Paring —
Wild Horse Pinot Noir

Ristorante Mamma Gina

❖ Veal Chop Milanese

SERVES 4

4   bone-in veal chops
6   eggs
2 ½ cups of breadcrumbs
½   cup of flour
2   lemons for garnish
Olive oil for pan-frying
Salt and freshly ground pepper

For over two decades Ristorante Mamma Gina has stood as a benchmark of authentic Tuscan cuisine and is well known for its tradition of elegant home style cooking. Owner Piero Pierattoni sets the tone, saying "We don't use anything but the very best and remain true to authentic recipes."

While every dish makes it clear that only the finest and freshest ingredients are used in each recipe, Executive Chef Tony Gonzales is showcasing his lightly breaded, pan fried Costoletta di vitella "Milanese" as a classic example of this fact.

The professional service staff proudly presents Chef Tony's creations with an unpretentious and gracious attitude. The informally elegant atmosphere is accented by soft earth tones, polished brass and rich splashes of color. An award-winning wine list and a number of decadent Italian desserts add to an authentic Tuscan experience.

Method —

In a shallow dish beat eggs and season with salt and pepper. Add flour into a separate shallow dish and breadcrumbs in a third. Using a meat mallet, carefully pound each veal chop, leaving bone attached to ⅓ of an inch or less. Season the veal with salt and pepper. Working with one piece of veal at a time, dip first in the flour, shaking off excess. Place the floured veal into the beaten eggs, coating completely. Place the veal into the breadcrumb mixture and gently press crumbs into the veal. Set a large plate, and continue with remaining veal slices.

In a large skillet with high sides, heat oil to 375°F. Cook on each side for about 1½ minutes or until golden brown. Serve with lemon wedges.

Note: The veal chop is delicious when accompanied with arugula salad (rocket salad), red onion and cherry tomatoes served in a lemon vinaigrette. Yet, any salad of choice will marry well with the Veal Chop Milanese.

Wine & Spirit Pairing —
Dolcetto D'alba by Andrea Oberto, Piemonte region of Italy

Shame on the Moon

❖ Bourbon Glazed Liver and Onions

SERVES **4**

8   3 ounce slices of calf's liver,
    ¼ inch thick each
2   medium white onions
2   tablespoons red wine
    vinegar
1   cup canola oil
4   tablespoons light brown
    sugar
1   cup bourbon
2   tablespoons tomato paste
½   cup beef or vegetable stock
4   tablespoons flour
Salt and white pepper

Here we have a real neighborhood favorite not only with the locals but also with those who pass through our valley regularly. There is a distinctive ambiance beginning with a genuine personal welcome and a sense of understated elegance that carries right though the entire evening. Decor is big city chic tempered with warm, cozy accents. Outstanding service and quality cuisine fondly referred to as "gourmet comfort food" awaits you. The eclectic menu ranges from Veal Meatloaf with Garlic Mash Potatoes to Seared Ahi Steak to Pasta and homemade desserts.

Chef Jorge's signature dish, Sautéed Calf's Liver with Onions & Bourbon Glaze, is renowned throughout the valley. Co-owners Chef Jorge Villabonas, Tom Tews and Milan Tojagic accredit their twenty three plus years of success to "hands-on management, attention to detail and guest recognition." "Our focus is on providing an outstanding dining experience that our guests enthusiastically share with their friends," says the trio.

Method —

Peel and slice onions and sauté in medium saucepan with 3 tablespoons of canola oil, until caramelized. Add red vinegar, 2 tablespoons of bourbon, 2 tablespoons of brown sugar, salt and pepper to taste. Sautee for another 3 minutes, set aside.

Dust the slices of calf's liver on both sides with a mixture of flour, 1 teaspoon salt and ½ teaspoon white pepper. In a large sauté pan, heat a ½ cup of canola oil until the oil becomes clear. Sauté on each side for 2 minutes over medium-high heat, remove liver slices and set aside. Discard oil.

Deglaze the pan with ½ cup of bourbon and flame until the flame subsides. Add beef or vegetable stock, tomato paste, 2 tablespoons light brown sugar and reduce for 2 minutes until glaze forms. Adjust seasoning with salt and pepper to taste.

Serve two slices of liver atop mashed potatoes on each plate. Top each serving with ¼ each of the caramelized onions and bourbon glaze. Optional, 2 slices of crisp bacon may be added. Serve with vegetables of your choice.

Note: The oil must be very hot so the liver sears and retains its juices for optimum quality. Use a pair of kitchen tongs so the liver is not pierced. Drop the liver slices in the hot oil and watch for splatters.

Wine & Spirit Pairing —
Any good red wine of your choice

The Steakhouse

Agua Caliente Casino · Resort · Spa

❖ Filet Oscar

Filet:
- 4   8 ounce filet mignon steaks
- 1   tablespoon Montréal steak seasoning or salt and pepper
- 8   ounces king crab meat
- 12   spears of medium sized asparagus
- 4   ounces black peppercorn demi glaze
- 1   tablespoon whole butter, room temperature

Béarnaise Sauce:
- ¼   cup fresh tarragon, chopped
- 2   shallots, minced
- ¼   cup champagne vinegar
- ¼   cup dry white wine
- 3   egg yolks
- 1   stick butter, melted

Salt and pepper to taste

For a truly spectacular dining experience, visit The Steakhouse. A *Wine Spectator* Award Winner, The Steakhouse boasts an extraordinary wine cellar, prime aged beef, succulent seafood and mouth-watering desserts. Every dish is created with loving care in an elegant, unhurried environment where haute cuisine and friendly and attentive service are a given.

Executive Chef Tim Wilcox chose to feature his Filet Oscar. This wonderful duo incorporates the most popular steak — filet mignon — and king crab legs. "My version of this dish expresses what's most important to me when I prepare any food — perfect ingredients," he says. What sets The Steakhouse apart from others is the all natural Prime Beef we order from a boutique grower with extremely high standards, consistent quality and marbling."

The Steakhouse at Agua Caliente Casino·Resort·Spa™ in Rancho Mirage is redefining spectacular!

Method —

Filet: Season steaks and broil over a hot BBQ or in oven to desired temperature. Steam crab meat and hold hot. Steam asparagus and hold hot.

Bearnaise Sauce: In a small saucepan, combine the tarragon, shallots, vinegar and wine over medium-high heat. Bring to a simmer and cook until reduced by half. Remove from heat and set aside. Place a stainless steel bowl in a saucepan containing simmering water, or use a double boiler. Whisk the egg yolks until doubled in volume. Slowly add the melted butter and continue beating until sauce is thickened. Stir in reserved shallot reduction. Season with salt and pepper and set aside wrapped in a warm spot. Hold at room temperature.

Prepare demi glaze as directed and hold hot. When steaks are at desired temperature, pull from heat and let rest for 2 minutes. Slice steaks horizontally one time to separate into 2 halves. Ladle 1-ounce of demi glaze in center of warm plate. Place one half of filet on plate. Place 2 ounces crab meat over this half. Place 3 spears of steamed asparagus on top of crab meat. Spoon béarnaise over asparagus. Place second half of filet over béarnaise. Using a pastry brush, brush butter over top of filet. Serve with garlic mashed potatoes.

Note: Demi glaze can be purchased at your neighborhood specialty grocery store.

Wine & Spirit Pairing —
2003 Rodney Strong Alexander's Crown Single Vineyard Cabernet

Stuft Pizza
Bar & Grill

SERVES 4

Salad:
- 3 large chicken breasts, grilled
- 2 large heads romaine lettuce
- ½ pound of mescaline baby greens
- 2 cups gorgonzola cheese crumbles
- 3 granny smith apples, diced into ½ inch cubes
- 1 pound red seedless grapes, destemmed
- 1 cup dried cranberries
- 1 cup candied walnuts

Dressing:
- 1½ ounces honey mustard dressing
- ½ tablespoon chipotle paste

Piadina:
- Focaccia or Artisan bread
- 2 cups shredded mozzarella or cheese of your choice
- Olive oil and chopped garlic cloves

❖ Summer Salad on Piadina

In 2004, Jack Bertram and his family opened Stuft Pizza® Bar & Grill, the newest franchise of their family-owned restaurants, in the heart of Old Town La Quinta. A success since it opened, the restaurant is surrounded by tall palm trees and mountain views, with two beautiful patios to enjoy. You can watch your favorite sports team inside on one of the restaurant's many plasma TVs, or pick up a pizza from their convenient curbside take-out entrance.

The special dish selected by the Bertrams is Summer Salad — their most popular menu item: "Once you try it, you're hooked," says Noelle. Stuft Pizza offers a great variety of food beyond their award-winning pizza. Try the Cajun Ahi appetizer, a delicious salad or pasta, prime N.Y. Steak or the delicious Seabass Picatta. Round out your selection with a hearty micro-brewed beer, specialty cocktail, or one of their great wines.

Method —

Lightly coat your focaccia or artisan bread with olive oil and garlic, sprinkle lightly with cheese, and bake for 8 to 10 minutes in 350°F oven. While your bread is cooking, dice grilled chicken breasts and green apples into half-inch cubes, and chop the heads of romaine into 1 inch squares. Combine all ingredients in a large mixing bowl except the candied walnuts. Add dressing and toss lightly. Remove bread from the oven and place tossed salad on top of the bread, while the bread is still hot. Add candied walnuts to the top of the salad.

Dressing: Blend dressing and chipotle paste together for 1 minute, in a blender. Don't overdue it, the dressing is potent.

Note: You will find the candied walnuts at any specialty grocery store, As for the piadina, ours is made with pizza dough, but we recommend choosing your favorite artisan, herb or focaccia bread from your local market. Many are so lively that you may not even need to add the garlic, olive oil, or cheese. One last hint: make sure to use chipotle paste and not whole chipotles — otherwise you will be in for some real fire in your mouth!

Wine & Spirit Pairing —
Sattui's Gamay Rouge

Jack Bertram

Trattoria Tiramisu

❖ Spaghetti Allo Scoglio

1 pound spaghetti
8 ounces black mussels, scrubbed
8 ounces manila clams, scrubbed
8 ounces calamari
8 ounces shrimp, cleaned
4 tablespoons extra virgin olive oil
½ cup white wine
2 teaspoons Italian parsley, freshly diced
6 whole cloves garlic, peeled and slightly pressed
Arugula
Cherry tomatoes
Crushed red pepper
Salt to taste
Grilled langoustine (optional garnish)

This intimate dining room offers genuine Italian hospitality where the tables are covered with white cloths and accented by soft candlelight. The walls are adorned with pictures of the Mediterranean countryside. Marika and Chef Mario Marfia greet you as if into their own home, and the rest of your dining experience is orchestrated by their knowledgeable and charming Italian speaking service staff.

Authentic Italian dishes in Mediterranean styles include pastas, fresh seafood specials and, on Saturday night, roasted leg of veal awaits you. Call ahead and Mario will prepare his lasagna or any of your favorites. Spaghetti allo Scoglio is their signature dish. "I was born and raised in Sicily, spending many years in the Mediterranean," says Chef Mario. "It is those cultural aspects I bring to my every day cooking. This dish represents that influence. You can taste the flavors and freshness throughout." As for its namesake, Tiramisu, save room for this surprisingly light and flavor-filled dessert.

Method —

Over medium-high heat, in a 12-14 inch sauté pan, add extra virgin olive oil, garlic and crushed red pepper. Sauté until garlic is golden brown. Add tomatoes, parsley, calamari, shrimp, mussels and clams, and white wine. Sauté about 3 to 5 minutes, stirring and tossing, until all of the shells have opened. In a 6-quart pan, bring water to boil add 2 tablespoons salt. Add 1 pound of spaghetti. It will take about 6 minutes to cook "al dente." Do not overcook the pasta.

Add cooked spaghetti into the sauce and let it cook for approximately 2 minutes. Finish it with chopped arugula and a touch of extra virgin olive oil.

Note: Use fresh, cleaned mussels, clams and shrimp. Discard any that have an open shell that won't close. Discard shells that failed to open when heated.

Wine & Spirit Pairing —
Terlato Chardonnay

Vicky's of Santa Fe

✦ Mango Salsa Sea Scallops

16 scallops, 10 to 12 ounces
3 tablespoons canola oil
1 teaspoon lemon juice
1 tablespoon fresh basil, diced
1 tablespoon thyme, diced
1 tablespoon chives, diced
1 tablespoon garlic, minced
2 cups loosely packed fresh
  baby spinach, 12 ounces

Mango Salsa:
2 ripe mangos, peeled and
  diced
1 small red bell pepper, diced
¼ small red onion, diced
Juice of 1 orange
Juice of 1 lime
Salt and pepper to taste
Pinch of fresh cilantro

On the dining scene in the desert since 1989, Vicky's offers Old-World adobe architecture, Mexican pavers, high ceilings, three separate dining rooms, and a piano bar where you can enjoy the talented Doug Montgomery on piano during the season.

Vicky's is known for generous portions of good quality food such as whole rotisserie chickens, 16 ounce New York strip steaks, 16 ounce center cut veal chops, and rack of New Zealand lamb. All of Vicky's New York strip steaks, prime rib steaks and filet mignon are Nebraska corn-fed. Vicky's also offers battered or sautéed tiger shrimp and a variety of fresh seasonal seafood complemented by local seasonal produce. Stop by the wine cellar boasting a wide range of California and well known boutique vintners. Their Mango Salsa Sea Scallops is our featured recipe.

Owner Marc Latliberte invites you to experience Vicky's combination of upscale, informal atmosphere, simplified menu and mouthwatering meals.

Method —

Mango Salsa: Combine ⅔ of the diced mango, red onion and bell pepper in a mixing bowl. In a blender, mix the rest of the mango with the orange and lime juice. Blend until puréed. Add all ingredients together. Mix well.

Scallops: Using a paper towel, pat scallops dry, season with salt and pepper. Heat 2 tablespoons of canola oil in a large skillet over medium heat. Add scallops, 4 per serving. Brown 3 minutes undisturbed. Turn and cook an additional 2 minutes adding basil, thyme, chives and garlic to taste. Remove from heat and set aside. Add the remaining canola oil to pan and cook the spinach 1 or 2 minutes. Portion spinach into 4 servings and transfer each to a plate. Top with mango salsa and place scallops on top. Season with lemon juice, salt and pepper to taste.

Note: Scallops are often soaked on a phosphate solution to prolong shelf life. Always ask for "dry" scallops to ensure they haven't been soaked.

Wine & Spirit Paring —
Santa Margherita Pinot Grigio

Wally's
Desert Turtle

2   Maine lobsters steamed,
    1 ½ pound each, shelled and
    sliced

Marinated Mango:
2   mangos sliced
2   shallots thinly sliced
1   bunch cilantro, dill or chervil
Dash of Tabasco
Salt and pepper
Juice of 1 lime

Vinaigrette:
2   tablespoons sweet chili
    paste
6   tablespoons extra virgin
    olive oil
Juice of 1 lime

❖ Lobster & Spicy Mango Salad

One word — Magnificent. This magnificent restaurant was built by Wally Botello, the founder of the famed Velvet Turtle chain, and for over 30 years has been owned and operated by his family.

Here we find unforgettable continental cuisine in one of the most exquisite restaurants in California. Wally's stands as the desert's most highly awarded restaurant as recipient of the prestigious *Mobil Travel Four Star*, *AAA Four Diamond*, and the *DiRoNA* awards, to name a few.

Entering over twinkling lights, you will be swept away by the spectacular design that sophisticated world cities would envy. The beveled mirrored ceilings, soft lighting, Peruvian artifacts and hand-painted murals create a warm and elegant ambiance in which to savor the flawless culinary creations of Executive Chef Pascal Lallemand,

Chef Pascal states "I love this Lobster & Marinated Mango Salad for many reasons. The lobster and spicy marinated mango work well together. It can be a nice winter appetizer or a summer main course."

Method —

Mix all ingredients together and refrigerate overnight.

Assembly: Mold the mango in a 3 inch ring or any other shape and display the sliced lobster tail on top. Drizzle vinaigrette around the salad and garnish with fresh micro greens, fresh chervil and the lobster claws.

Note: Use fresh live lobsters. They can be cooked, shelled and refrigerated the day before. Parts of the shell may be used as plate decoration. For a 1½ pound lobster the boiling time is 10 minutes. Remove from boiling water and set aside to cool before refrigerating.

Wine and Spirit Pairing —
A Riesling or a Sylvaner nicely chilled

Zin

American Bistro

SERVES **4**

Lamb:
2   racks of lamb, 25 ounces each, Frenched
½   cup bread crumbs
¼   cup melted butter
1   tablespoon minced parsley
1   tablespoon Dijon mustard
1   head of garlic, broken into cloves
2   tablespoons extra virgin olive oil

Orange Sauce:
1   sprig of fresh thyme
1   sprig of fresh tarragon
½   cup orange juice
1   large tomato, chopped
1   cup chicken stock
Salt and black pepper to taste

Flageolets Beans:
1   cup flageolet beans, soaked overnight
1   bouquet garni (thyme, parsley, bay leaf, clove)
½   cup each of onion, carrot, and celery, diced
1   tablespoon of tomato paste
1   teaspoon minced garlic
2   tablespoons olive oil
3   cups cold water or chicken broth

Haricots Vert (Green Beans)

 ## Roast Rack of Lamb

Just as the Zinfandel grape is uniquely American, so is Zin American Bistro. While the skillfully prepared cuisine is where everything starts, Owner/Chef Nicolas Klontz doesn't stop here. The wine list has been honored with the *Wine Spectator Award of Excellence* two years in a row. High energy, friendly surroundings and attentive but unobtrusive service complete the picture.

Nicolas was classically trained in the "Old Country" using traditional European techniques. He presents his creations with an artful flair. Fresh, seasonal ingredients cause his innovative American comfort foods to take center stage. Nicolas' lifelong companion, Mindy Reed, has not only developed their notable wine program but personally creates all the incredible desserts. Chef Nicolas selected Roasted Rack of Lamb. He fondly recalls the rave reviews it began generating years ago in his restaurant in Spa, Belgium, when he first prepared it for Master Chef Roger Vergé for his son's christening.

Method —

Flageolet Beans: Heat olive oil and sauté garlic and vegetables 5 minutes over medium heat. Stir in tomato paste and cook a few minutes more. Add soaked beans, season with salt and pepper. Add bouquet garni and bring to a boil. Lower heat to low and simmer until beans are cooked. Add water if needed.

Lamb: Preheat oven to 400°F. Trim the lamb racks of any extra fat. Separate the garlic head into cloves but do not peel. Place them in a small sauté pan and roast in oven for 30 minutes or until golden and soft. Spread mustard on top of lamb. Sprinkle with thyme, salt and pepper. Pat gently. Mix together the breadcrumbs, melted butter and parsley. Pat firmly onto rubbed side of lamb. Heat enough olive oil to lightly cover the bottom of an oven-proof skillet large enough to hold the lamb over medium-high to high heat. Place lamb in pan and quickly brown on each side, about 4 minutes per side. Place pan in oven and roast for about 20 minutes or until meat thermometer registers 135°F for medium-rare. Remove from pan. Set aside and keep warm. Drain fat from roasting pan and deglaze with orange juice. Add chopped tomatoes, sprig of thyme and tarragon. Reduce liquid by half. Add roasted garlic, chicken broth and season with salt and pepper. Reduce by half again, strain and whisk in cold butter.

Assemble and Serve: Place flageolet beans on warm plates. Top with sautéed Haricots Vert. Slice lamb racks and place on top of the vegetables. Spoon a little sauce around.

Wine & Spirit Pairing —
Rosenblum Rockpile Zinfandel

Centuries ago, sommeliers cellared, selected, and served wines to royalty. Eventually the tradition of the sommelier spread to restaurants, where such an individual is expected to have extensive knowledge of wines and their suitability with various dishes. The chefs featured in our book have offered a wine or spirit pairing to accompany their dish. Now you can feel like royalty with your own personal sommelier.

Vino 100 is a relaxing environment where you can explore the world of wine. The 25-foot granite tasting bar is a perfect space to sample great wines from around the world, while meeting new friends or old. Here you will find an unpretentious staff of knowledge people that truly appreciate wine. Proprietors Brian and Michelle Estenson, sister Marilyn Estenson and their team will help guide you in selecting the perfect wine to present when you prepare one of *"Savor A Taste's"* signature dishes in your home.

Vino 100
Featured Wine Sommelier

Wine and Food Pairing Guide

	SAUVIGNON BLANC	CHARDONNAY	RIESLING	PINOT NOIR	SYRAH	MERLOT	CABERNET SAUVIGNON	ZINFANDEL
CHEESES & NUTS	Feta Goat Cheese Pine Nuts	Asiago Havarti Almonds	Havarti Gouda Candied Walnuts	Goat Cheese Brie Walnuts	Sharp Cheddar Roquefort Hazelnuts	Parmesan Romano Chestnuts	Cheddar Gorgonzola Walnuts	Brie Aged Cheese
MEAT OR FOWL	Chicken Turkey	Veal Chicken Pork	Smoked Sausage Duck	Lamb Sausage Filet Mignon Chicken	Roast Game Pepperoni Spicy Sausage	Grilled Meats Steak	Venison Rib Eye Beef Stew	Pork Spicy Sausage Beef Duck
SEAFOOD	Sole Oysters Scallops	Halibut Shrimp Crab	Sea Bass Trout	Orange Roughy Tuna	Salmon	Grilled Swordfish Tuna	Grilled Tuna	Cioppino Blackened Fish
VEGETABLES & FRUIT	Citrus Green Apple Asparagus	Potato Apple Squash Mango	Apricots Chili Peppers Pears	Mushrooms Dried Fruit Figs Strawberries	Currants Stewed Tomatoes Beets	Caramelized Onions Tomatoes Plums	Black Cherries Broccoli Tomatoes	Cranberries Grilled Peppers Eggplant
HERB & SPICES	Chives Tarragon Cilantro	Tarragon Sesame Basil	Rosemary Ginger	Nutmeg Cinnamon Clove	Oregano Sage	Mint Rosemary Juniper	Rosemary Juniper Lavender	Pepper Nutmeg
SAUCES	Citrus Light Sauces	Cream Sauce Pesto	Sweet Bbq Spicy Chutney	Mushroom Sauce Light-Medium Red Sauce	Heavy Sauce Red Sauce Barbeque	Bolognese Béarnaise	Brown Sauce Tomato Sauce	Spicy Cajun Salsa
DESSERTS	Sorbet Key Lime Pie	Banana Bread Vanilla Pudding	Apple Pie Caramel Sauce	Crème Brûlée White Chocolate	Black Forest Cake Rhubarb Pie	Dark Chocolate Berries Fondue	Bittersweet Chocolate Espresso Gelato	Spice Cake Gingerbread Carrot Cake

**Adobe Grill
at La Quinta Resort & Club**
49-499 Eisenhower Drive
La Quinta, CA 92253
760.564.5725
www.laquintaresort.com

Amoré Ristorante Italiano
47-474 Washington Street
La Quinta, CA 92253
760.777.1315
www.amore-dining.com

Arnold Palmer's
78-164 Avenue 52
La Quinta, CA 92253
760.771.4653
www.arnoldpalmers.net

**AZUR
at La Quinta Resort & Club**
49-499 Eisenhower Drive
La Quinta, CA 92253
760.564.7600
www.laquintaresort.com

Babe's Bar-B-Que
Restaurant & Brewhouse
71-800 Highway 111
Rancho Mirage, CA 92270
760.346.8738

Babe's Jack-A-Lope Ranch
80-400 Highway 111
Indio, CA 92201

Café des Beaux-Arts
73-640 El Paseo
Palm Desert, CA 92260
760.346.0669
www.cafedesbeauxarts.com

Castelli's Ristorante
73-098 Highway 111
Palm De sert, CA 92260
760.773.3365

**Chez Pierre
An Authentic French Bistro**
44-250 Town Center Way
Palm Desert, CA 92260
760.346.1818
www.chezpierrebistro.com

Cunard's Sandbar
78-120 Calle Tampico
La Quinta, CA 92247
760.564.3660

Copley's On Palm Canyon
621 North Palm Canyon Drive
Palm Springs, CA 92262
760.327.9555
www.copleysrestaurant.com

Exquisite Desserts
Phone for Ordering Information
760.772.5522
www.exquisitedesserts.net

**The Falls Prime Steakhouse
& Martini Bar**
155 South Palm Canyon Drive
Palm Springs, CA 92260
760.416.8664
www.thefallsprimesteakhouse.com

The Falls Prime Steakhouse & Martini Bar
78-430 Highway 111
La Quinta, CA 92253
760.777.9999
www.thefallsprimesteakhouse.com

Firecliff Contemporary California Cuisine
73-725 El Paseo
Palm Desert, CA 92260
760.773.6565
www.firecliffdining.com

Fusion One 11 Martini & Tapas Restaurant
73-850 Highway 111
Palm Desert, CA 92260
760.341.5903
www.fusionone11.com

Guillermo's Restaurante
72-850 El Paseo
Palm Desert, CA 92260
760.341.0980
www.restauranteguillermos.com

Le Basil Southeast Asian Cuisine
72-695 Highway 111
Palm Desert, CA 92260
760.773.1112

Lord Fletcher Inn
70-385 Highway 111
Rancho Mirage, CA 92270
760.328.1161
www.lordfletcher.com

Los Pepes Mexican Grill
73-091 Country Club Drive
Palm Desert, CA 92260
760.779.8977

Matchbox Vintage Pizza Bistro
155 S. Palm Canyon Drive
Palm Springs, CA 92262
760.778.6000
www.matchboxpalmsprings.com

McGowan's Irish Inn
73-340 Highway 111
Palm Desert, CA 92260
760.346.6032

The Nest
75-188 Highway 111
Indian Wells, CA 92210
760.346.2314
www.gotothenest.com

Paseo Palms Bar and Grill
73-040 El Paseo
Palm Desert, CA 92260
760.837.3800
www.paseopalms.com

Piero's Acqua Pazza California Bistro
71-800 Highway 111
Rancho Mirage, CA 92270
760.862.9800
www.pierosacquapazza.com

Purple Palm at Colony Palms Hotel
572 North Indian Canyon Drive
Palm Springs, CA 92262
760.969.1818
www.colonypalmshotel.com/dining

Red Tomato Original House of Lamb
68-784 East Palm Canyon
Cathedral City, CA 92234
760.328.7518
www.theredtomatoonline.com

Riccio's Italian
2155 North Palm Canyon Drive
Palm Springs, CA 92262
760.325.2369
www.riccios-palmsprings.com

Riccio's Steak & Seafood
495 North Palm Canyon Drive
Palm Springs, CA 92262
760.325.3111
www.ricciossteakandseafood.com

The Right Bank
70-065 Highway 111
Rancho Mirage, CA 92270
760.202.9380
www.desertnetwork.com/rightbank

Ristorante Mamma Gina
73-705 El Paseo
Palm Desert, CA 92260
760.568.9898
www.mammagina.com

Shame on the Moon
69-950 Frank Sinatra Drive
Rancho Mirage, CA 92270
760.324.5515
www.shameonthemoon.com

The Steakhouse
at Agua Caliente Casino · Resort · Spa
32-250 Bob Hope Drive
Rancho Mirage, CA 92270
888.999.1995
www.hotwatercasino.com

Stuft Pizza Bar & Grill
Old Town La Quinta
78-015 Main Street
La Quinta, CA 92253
760.777.9989
www.stuftpizza.com/laquinta

Trattoria Tiramisu
72-655 Highway 111
Palm Desert, CA 92260
760.773.9100

Vicky's of Santa Fe
45-100 Club Drive
Indian Wells, CA 92210
760.345.9770
www.vickysofsantafe.com

Vino 100
68-718 East Palm Canyon Drive
Cathedral City, CA 92234
760.321.5478
www.vino100cc.com

Wally's Desert Turtle
71-775 Highway 111
Rancho Mirage, CA 92270
760.568.9321
www.wallys-desert-turtle.com

Zin American Bistro
198 South Palm Canyon Drive
Palm Springs, CA 92262
760.322.6300
www.zinamericanbistro.com

Tasting Notes

APPETIZERS

Duck, Roasted Breast of Duckling, **37**

Scallop and Sea Bass, Crispy Duo, **57**

Tuna, Ahi Tartar Tower, **33**

SALADS

Broiled Hanger Steak, Heirloom Tomatoes, **25**

Lobster & Spicy Mango Salad, **79**

Summer Salad on Piadina, **73**

MEAT

Beef Stew, Caldillo Duranguerio, **45**

Filet Oscar, **71**

Lamb Chops, Grilled Toluca Style, **9**

Lamb, Roast Rack & Orange Sauce, **81**

Lamb Shank, **49**

Liver & Onions, Bourbon Glazed, **69**

Osso Buco Alla Milanese & Saffron Risotto, **61**

Pork Chop Sunset Strip, **65**

Pork Tenderloin, Hickory Smoked & Cole Slaw, **17**

Short Ribs, Braised, **43**

Veal Chop Milanese, **67**

POULTRY

Chicken'n Dumplings, **59**

Chicken, Thai Satay, **41**

Duck Magret, Fresh Fig Sauce, **21**

Pollo All'Arancio, **23**

Turkey Chili & Skillet Corn Bread, **19**

PASTA

Cannelloni, Stuffed Veal & Chicken, **51**

Spaghetti Allo Scoglio, **75**

SEAFOOD

Allo Scoglio, Spaghetti, **75**

Chilean Sea Bass, **13**

Lobster Gnocchi, **11**

Monkfish, Hoisin-Ginger Glazed, **35**

Onaga Wrapped In Pancetta, **27**

Salmon en Papillote, **55**

Salmon, Braised Irish, Sweet Potato Gnocchi, **15**

Sea Scallops, Citrus Soy, **47**

Sea Scallops, Mango Salsa, **77**

Seafood, Mixed Mediterranean Grill, **63**

Shrimp *"Billye"* **29**

Shrimp, Camarones a la Calafia, **39**

SWEET TREATS

Lemon Curd Tart with Raspberries, **31**

Orange Brûléed French Toast, **53**

WINE & SPIRIT REFERENCE

Wine Sommelier, **83**

A THANK YOU NOTE

There are so many people we would like to acknowledge for their inspiration, enthusiasm, support, commitment and friendship.

Our gifted graphic designer, Thomas Granade, has educated us about design, and made sure that we had fun along the way. A book like this doesn't happen overnight. This has been a process of many months of design and creative development. Thomas has been there from the beginning, giving us encouragement and direction. Because of his insight, the vision for the next edition of *Savor A Taste* will soar even higher. We thank him for his spirit and generosity.

Thanks to photographer extraordinaire, Mark Cieslikowski, for his fine photography and expertise to make the book the exquisite presentation that it is today. Mark went the extra mile to complete our vision and was patient enough to incorporate our passion in those images when he could have said that it was "good enough."

And, special thanks goes to Gayl Biondi, the consulting editor, for her availability and help with all the final details that were needed to finish this project on time.

We would like to thank those restaurants that contributed their signature dishes. These talented individuals shared their dreams and opened their doors offering some of the best dining experiences.

And, finally, to our families and friends for their encouragement on our journey. Thank you for your love, support and prayers.

Victoria & Kim